OVER **100**
S&M
SEX TIPS

THIS IS A CARLTON BOOK

Text and design copyright © Carlton Books
Limited 2008

This edition published by
Carlton Books Limited
20 Mortimer Street
London W1T 3JW

ISBN 978 1 84732 201 2

Printed and bound in Malaysia

Senior Executive Editor: Lisa Dyer
Senior Art Editor: Gülen Shevki-Taylor
Design: Zoë Dissell
Production: Kate Pimm

OVER 100 S&M SEX TIPS

LISA SUSSMAN

CARLTON
BOOKS

1 HOUSE RULES

Power games are part and parcel of any relationship. They only get you in hot water when you regularly play outside of the bedroom. But a little control between the sheets? That's a whole different shebang. As long as your partner is game, these little ploys can give your sex life a kick. And they're a lot quicker and easier to do than most Kama Sutra moves.

Before you start mastering your slipknot (thread down to Tip 56), you need to swot up on the rules of the game. Most people think of S&M as no-holds-barred, anything-goes sex play. But getting tied up, whipped, handcuffed, or even mercilessly tickled requires some basic guidelines to keep things safe and sexy. Here's everything you need to know before getting down to business.

IS YOUR PARTNER GAME?

Even if you've been together for longer than the Rolling Stones, you may not want to suddenly whisper in your partner's ear a sweet nothing à la 'I've always dreamt of being strapped to the bed, covered in whipped cream and lashed by your tongue'. Here's your step-by-step guide to getting the conversation started.

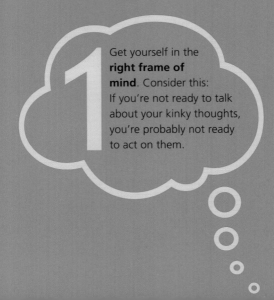

1

Get yourself in the **right frame of mind**. Consider this: If you're not ready to talk about your kinky thoughts, you're probably not ready to act on them.

2 **Start simple.** Even if your ultimate fantasy is to create a home dungeon of bondage equipment, start by getting out a few scarves during your next romp and study your partner's reaction. If they seem freaked, they are probably more likely to come around if they think it's their idea. So claim that you were hoping to re-enact the Dance of the Seven Veils – but now that *they* brought it up, it might be fun to try a little tie-up scenario.

3 When you're ready to dive deeper, **show rather than tell.** There's a magazine for every desire under the sun. Try leaving one or two lying around (the bedside table is a good place) and thumb through them with your lover.

The 'a friend of mine' gambit. This also works when you want to be subtle: 'A friend of mine went out with this guy who liked to spank her lightly on the bottom and she said it was surprisingly sexy.' 'A friend of a friend got pissed the other night and said that he's really into being tied up by his girlfriend.'

4

Along the same lines, **use a study:** 'I read the other day that one out of every ten people has experimented with sadomasochism' (true by the way) 'and that S&M is most popular among educated, middle- and upper-middle-class men and women' (also true) 'and that getting into kink shows that you're really comfortable with your sexuality and knowing what gets you off' (yup, also true) 'and that S&M is like a cardio workout.' Okay, this last one is a bit of an exaggeration – you will burn more calories when you play rough because doing anything new jumpstarts your adrenalin, which in turn makes your heart pump harder. But how much you work it depends on your fitness level in the first place.

Be prepared to **bust stereotypes.** S&M is not just for leather-clad gay boys and whip-whacking dominatrices. Nor is S&M just another way of saying you're in an abusive relationship. Kinsey reported that many couples include horseplay in their lovemaking – slapping, light spanking, mild biting, teasing, tickling torture and pinching. Now that's vanilla sex with a cherry on top.

Just do it. This takes guts and you may want to wait for a special occasion such as a birthday or Valentine's Day before getting decked out in your strap-on dildo.

S&M CODE BOOK

Everything you need to talk the talk and walk the walk. If you don't swot up on the language, you may end up with a boner where you don't want it. Here's a who's who in the S&M world.

Top: This is the person in charge of the games. AKA Dom, Dominant, Master/Mistress.

Bottom: This is the person who gets to lie back and take it. AKA Sub, Submissive, Slave.

Switch: When you like to play both ways.

SM: Sadomasochism – as in 'It feels so good when I hurt you/It feels so good when you hurt me.'
Insider tip: You call it 'S and M' only if you don't do it or if you experiment only occasionally with those handcuffs you keep hidden at the back of the bedside cabinet. If, on the other hand, you own not only handcuffs but also a spanking bench, a flogger, some paraffin wax, an unbreakable Pyrex dildo and various other unmentionables – you simply call it SM. S&M is Madonna in kinky outfits. SM is hardcore.

BSDM: Short for Bondage, Discipline, Sadism and Masochism, this is the new politically correct tech term for good old-fashioned SM. Other popular abbreviations include D&S (Dominance and Submission) and B&D (Bondage and Dominance/Discipline). Yabadabadoo!

24/7: Ooh, I need your love, babe – you're into a full-time erotic power exchange 24 hours a day, 7 days a week.

SSC: No, not Sizzling, Sexy Cunnilingus – it means Safe, Sane and Consensual.

Squick: You've reached your limit and need to say the 'safe' word (make a risk-free jump to Tip 11).

TPE: Total Power Exchange (think collar, leash and licking boots).

Wearing the right (or wrong) **coloured handkerchief** can lead to hanky panky. Slipping in a coloured cloth so that it partially hangs out of your back pocket signals that you are game to play – right pocket means you're a Sub, left pocket means you're a Dom and both pockets indicate you'll swing either way (if you've already forgotten what these terms mean, see Tip 8).

Scan opposite to see which colour flag you should be flying to coordinate with your mood. Be warned – you'll need to know your shades. Shops selling **Hanky Code** bandanas commonly give away free key charts, but studies have shown that women recognize far more specific terms than men – describing items as 'mauve' or 'aubergine', say, rather than simply 'purple'. The Hanky Code makes such fine distinctions as gold, rust and apricot, and similar shades signal far-from-similar passions. Mix up your fuchsia and your dark red and instead of a light spanking, you'll find yourself being used as a human hand puppet. Twice over.

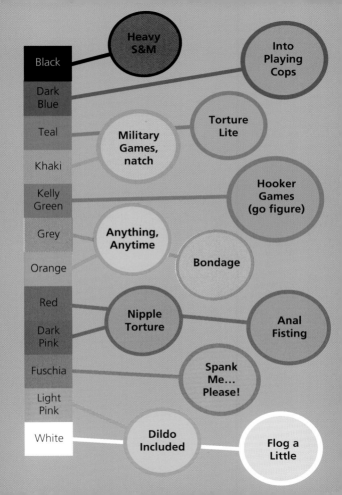

Before you get down to having hot kinky sex, **you both need to agree** on what kind of hot kinky sex you want to have. Yeah, it takes away some of the thrill of the moment, but so does the shock of having your partner slap a muzzle on you and start commanding you to beg – if that's not what you had in mind, that is. So decide before you play the following.

11

- **Who is in charge.**
- **What the scene is.** Is spanking okay or just a light tap? Is it okay if you pretend to be a meter maid whipping his sorry butt for illegally parking? Can he visit your back door?

- **What your safe word is** – these are phrases for telling your lover to either slow down or stop altogether. Think of them as your emergency brakes for when things get too tough, too scary, too painful, too annoying or simply too silly or boring. Plain old 'Stop' doesn't work as the other person could interpret it as, 'Stop, oh stop, that feels so good, you're the best…' Think of words you normally wouldn't moan between the sheets, such as 'Pukka' and 'Whatev-ah'. It's important that when the code word is used, all action stops immediately.

SOS

Accidents happen.
Here's how to apply first
aid. No CPR necessary.

- **Avoid anything that puts any pressure AT ALL on the front of the neck.** It can quickly lead to unconsciousness, as the carotid arteries go right to the brain.
- *Never, ever, ever* strike the head, neck, **lower back (where the kidneys are), chest, backs of knees or abdomen.** Continued internal (rather than superficial) pain several hours after a love session may indicate serious damage. Visit the doctor.
- **Be careful with gags** or very tight laces: Anything that restricts breathing can lead to suffocation – which is obviously not a good thing.
- If a position causes **dizziness or nausea**, stop and change direction – if you've been sitting, lie down; if you've been lying down, slowly sit up. This can also be a symptom of too-high temperatures, so lower the heat.

You can't make an omelette without breaking eggs. And you can't take part in a heavy-duty pain scene and not expect to get black and blue. In order of **bruising**: surprisingly whipping seldom causes marks, spanking sometimes does, caning always does and bondage does more than you'd think. You can avoid bondage bruises easily by covering the skin first before you put the ropes around and by taking care when releasing your partner (pulling rope over the skin may 'burn' it). As for marks caused by hitting, try sticking to well-padded areas like the bottom, thighs and back if any substantial force is being used.

14

Cold, blue or white limbs are not an S&M fashion statement. They can be caused by a too-tight rope or a strap, by compressing certain veins or arteries with the weight of the body, or because the hands have been over the head for too long. It's not as scary as it looks (the average arm, leg, hand or foot can do without blood for 45 minutes) but it may be uncomfortable in a not-sexy way. Remove all restraints so the blood flow can resume (a little light massage never hurts at this point). And never leave clamps, rings or weights on for longer than 15 minutes.

A jammed bolt is the bad dream of anyone who takes part in a lock-up scene. The main thing is not to panic. Try a few more times. If you're still stuck, don't use a saw. Instead, soap up the skin – you may be able to slip out of your tight spot. Otherwise, you'll need a pair of wire cutters (available from most do-it-yourself stores). For more on how to avoid getting locked-in next time, check out your cuff options under Tip 26.

Bad Dream Number 2 is the possibility of **losing something up the bum**. Most things will make their own way out given the chance (you could try taking a laxative to ease things along). Avoid this in the future by never inserting anything all the way. And while you're at it, never insert anything that is sharp-edged or breakable and always use plenty of juice (see Tips 39–41 for matching your grease to your action). If there's more than a spot of blood and/or pain after anal play, you'll need to get yourself medically checked out.

17

The
**burns from
wax drips** can
feel sizzling sexy – or
they may make you scream
'Ye-ouch!' To stop wax from getting
too hot, always use plain paraffin candles
or ones specifically made for dripping on
to the body (rather than the kind made
for creating atmosphere in a room). If
the temperature of your play gets too
blistering, cool the burned area with cold
water (*not* ice – it will add to the burn)
for one minute or more; don't apply petroleum
products or any greasy lotions or butter.

Make sure that you have a **safe hand signal** if you're using gags (see Tip 11 for more on playing safe). This way, the person being muzzled can still let their partner know if the rope is too tight or the clamps are pinching or they want to stop. Some people hold a hanky – if they drop it, that means stop. Others use a bell, apply hand squeezes or raise a pre-agreed finger.

Warning: None of the above should be considered medical advice.

18

TOYS 'R' LUST

It's playtime. Toys are not a must when it comes to making the scene, but they do make your games more fun (see Tip 55 for the lowdown on budget play). Read on for a few of a kinkster's favourite things – oh, such pretty packages tied up with string!

Remember that bondage equipment is not like a cheap pair of pantyhose – one size fits all. While you can certainly improvise with a handy roll of duct tape and a ball of twine, you may want to work with slightly more erotic materials specifically made for the moment.

Also, cuffs and lubes are *must-haves* that no self-respecting S&M player would be seen without.

BLINDFOLDS

Is love blind?

19

You knew those **silk scarves** you get from Auntie every year for your birthday were going to come in handy. Tie them with a simple fisherman's knot (loop down to Tip 57).

20

Although they come in a variety of materials, **leather eye coverings** are traditional. Make sure yours has a Velcro backing so you can adjust the size and get in and out easily. Lined blindfolds will be easier on your lids. To really dress the part, opt for one with studs.

21

Hoods take the blindfold idea one step further. Definitely not for beginners, the feeling of being enclosed may cause instant submission – but it can just as easily create out-and-out panic. Make the plunge with care.

GAGS

Don't say a word. If you're new to S&M, though, it's wise to avoid gags to start with, so that you can communicate easily with your partner.

Make sure you choose breathable fabric and never use gags when the wearer has a stuffed nose (you figure it out). Also remember to **establish a safe hand signal** (see Tip 18) in case the one being gagged wants to stop play. You can try speciality gags like cock gags (and yes, lads, they do come in different lengths) and ball gags (exactly what it sounds like).

ROPE & SCARF RESTRAINTS

There are loads of ways to get a grip, so don't hold back.

Many different lines of rope are available, but the best for newbies is a **solid braided nylon or cotton rope**. These are strong and, unlike synthetics, won't rub the skin the wrong way; slightly burn the edges of the nylon first so it doesn't fray. They'll also hold knots well and can be easily washed – yes, you should scrub-a-dub-dub your rope. Would you wear your undies again without a wash?

Keep your rope coiled so you can easily use it. It also helps to cut your ropes to specific lengths and mark them so you can quickly find which length you need chop-chop. If you can't remember your scouts training, study the knots in Tips 56–58.

25

Scarves don't actually make great restraints because soft materials tend to tighten under tension, occasionally getting so tight that they need to be cut off. If you must use a scarf, make sure it's not a favourite and keep a pair of scissors nearby in case you get into a tight spot.

CUFFS

Typical cuff materials are leather, rubber and nylon/cotton blends. Unless ultra-pain is your thing, pick up a lined pair so you don't get cuff burns and be sure to **check the fit**. It's not enough to check that your cuffs go around your ankle or wrist or testicles – you need to make sure they're tight enough so you can't slip out, but not so tight that you cut off circulation.

For **arm binders**, think long gloves pulled over both arms and buckle so that the arms are tied behind the back. They also come in rigid splints. An easier variation on the theme are **biceps binders**, which go just around the upper arm and across the back, so hands are left free.

Police-style handcuffs seem the obvious choice for booking a bondage scene with your partner in crime but most end up locking in place or shifting during your fun and games – or you lose the key. Instead, opt for **Velcro restraints** (which allow quick and easy break-outs), check out **faux-fur cuffs** that can be colour-coordinated with your outfit, or try cushy **leather straps that buckle** into place.

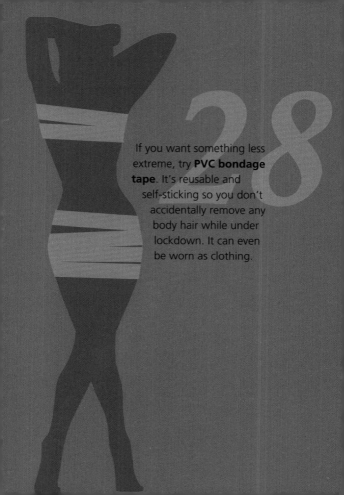

28

If you want something less extreme, try **PVC bondage tape**. It's reusable and self-sticking so you don't accidentally remove any body hair while under lockdown. It can even be worn as clothing.

If your bed doesn't have posts, you can still get the spread-eagled look you want by wrapping straps around the legs of the bed. Or try **sports sheets**

29

(think mattress sheets with a nylon cuff in each corner) – just remember to change your sheets before Granny pays a visit.

HARNESSES

Like a more elaborate type of strap, harnesses tie around the body. You can get them in traditional leather, chain, rubber and even parachute material for lounging-at-home bondage nights. Some have an open back, with straps down the sides, or a closed back, where the straps cross over. They're usually adjustable to a certain degree but you should **know your measurements to get a better fit**. Choose a bra or lower-body harness for a half-trussed look. All styles can come with an attachment for a cock ring or strap-on dildo.

30

Like edgier his 'n' hers outfits, harnesses come in **Top and Bottom versions** (for your lingo lowdown, see Tip 8). The Tops often have straps criss-crossing the chest while the Bottoms have the chest straps plus extra lengths for a cock ring or to go around the love triangle.

Cock and ball harnesses are like cock rings but the strap goes around his meat and two veg. Some have studs and padlocks, but even the most basic kind will help sustain staying power. To get him to snap one on, whisper in his ear that it turns an average *wiener* into a supersized sausage.

31

DRESS TO IMPRESS
Look the part with S&M wear.

32

Corsets, in the BSDM world, are designed not to create hourglass curves but to restrict movement. Usually made of latex, PVC or leather, they almost always have lots of laces and zippers to tighten things even more and some rings to keep the wearer tied in place.

33

A **collar** can be as simple as a necklace or choker, a standard dog collar or a metal, leather, PVC or leather neck band specially made to restrict movement. This last kind usually comes with a metal ring to attach a leash. They may buckle or fasten with Velcro.

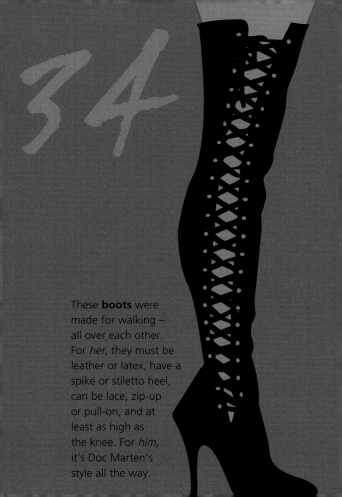

34

These **boots** were made for walking – all over each other. For *her*, they must be leather or latex, have a spike or stiletto heel, can be lace, zip-up or pull-on, and at least as high as the knee. For *him*, it's Doc Marten's style all the way.

JOY BUZZERS
Shock yourself with pleasure.

Beat your bedfellow into a quivering heap without laying a finger on them with the OhMiBod Boditalk **Escort Vibrator** (www. ohmibod.com). A call to your mobile phone triggers this discreet bullet vibrator that stays active for the length of your chat. It elevates phone sex from hokey to high-tech.

Another take on the absent-but-there theme is the **Je Joue** (www.jejoue.com), which is controlled remotely via e-mailed instructions that manoeuvre the textured, circular tip while you're video-chatting.

Get electrified with the **Violet Wand** (www.violetwand.org), a hand-held generator that comes complete with several glass and metal attachments. Depending on how much power is juiced through them, they produce anywhere from a tingling sensation to a full-blown shock to the system.

The **Octopus** is remote-control fun that no Dom should be without – it's a completely silent, soft silicone cock ring massager.

LUBES

Clean up your act
with the right lubricant
for the job.

39

For anything anal, **silicone-based lubes**
are slick and slippery-doo-da and stay
that way longer. This is because they're
not water soluble and therefore don't
get absorbed into the skin. What it all
adds up to is fewer applications and no
sticky gloopiness. Another nice bonus is
that silicone lubes don't block pores, so
there's less potential for bottom spots.
One drawback, though, is that they can be
harder to clean up.

40

Get a burn: try **warming lubes**, which heat up as you rub them on.

41

For anything involving the mouth, **edible lubes** will go down better. To smooth your play, check out some of Doc Johnson's Doc's Cocktails (www.docjohnson.com), which come in five mixed-drink flavours.

Warning: Oil-based lubes (such as massage oil, soap or cooking oils) are to be avoided as they corrode latex protection and leave behind a coating that can lead to infections.

WHIP IT UP

These tips may help you
decide what to use to
pack a wallop.

42

Ticklers are sticks with
feathers at the end. Use
your imagination.

43

A **crop** is a small (usually leather) whip.
Some crops come with a narrow flat
'flapper' on one end of a flexible shaft for
that oh-so-sexy tickle/whip combo. All you
need is a flick of the wrist to power one.

44

Canes come in a wide variety, from the domestic (usually straight and made from bamboo) to the schoolmaster's cane (a curved handle and more traditional). Novice spankers should work with shorter equipment – no longer than 1 m (3 feet) – to hone their accuracy and speed. Thicker canes cut the skin less often but cause more bruising. Thin canes cause more of a stinging feeling than the thud effect of their larger counterparts. It's your choice.

A **switch** is simply a cane that has been split at the bottom end to produce a fork or two tongues.

45

The word
'flogging'
may conjure
up images
of pirates
punishing
scallywags bound to
the mizzenmast – which is one
way to get into some scrummy role play.
Basically, a **flogger** is any whipping device
with a number of leather 'tails' or falls tied
together to a handle, which is covered with
braided leather. There are lots of variations,
but the important differences are the type
and weight of the leather used for the tails
and how their tips are shaped. Deerskin
leather, for example, is very light and soft,
making it almost impossible to do much, if
any, injury, while bison and bull leather are
heavy duty. The most common flogger is
the **cat-o-nine tails**; its nine tails are often
braided and end in a plain or knotted tip.

Whips are anything with one tail (see Tip 46 on floggers). Real ones can inflict pretty serious damage and are best left to the experts – like bronco busters. If you really want to beat it, try a specially made kind that doesn't hurt, no matter how hard it's swung. Some – like one called the 'Latex Whip on a Stick' – even sound painful when they come into contact with the skin, but are more likely to make you sigh than cry. Foam rounders or baseball bats also guarantee a soft, satisfying landing.

A **slapper** has a flat (usually leather) surface with another hinged flap of leather attached to it so that it makes an extra loud noise upon impact – think sexy sound effects. Some are lined with fleece on the receiving end to cushion the blow. They're small, so you can easily carry one for whenever and wherever the impulse strikes.

49

Start out with a **small paddle or riding crop**, which is easy to guide and more accurate than a flogger or whip. You won't lose your power punch – even lightweight ones can make it uncomfortable for someone to sit down for days.

CLAMPS, CLIPS, CRUSHERS & COCK RINGS

Pinch yourself – then read these tips for how to put the squeeze on.

Clamps are pretty much what they sound like: devices used for gripping onto various body parts such as nipples, balls and vaginal lips. Some nipple clamps are designed simply to give a light nip or a pull. Some are intended to produce a heavy pinch. And some actually have teeth on them that do a biting thing. The crème de la crème are vibrating clamps that give a full-body pinch and buzz. Nipple-to-vulva/penis clamps connect all of your best bits.

Clips are small devices that grip onto different areas of the body, like BSDM bling for the clitoris, nipples, labia and penis. They usually come in heavy metals like gold and silver, and may be topped with rhinestones and – sigh – mini vibrators.

A word of advice: Test the clamp on the wrist or less sensitive piece of skin first before using it on a sensitive area.

Cock rings are worn at the base of the penis to keep him going like a Duracell bunny. They come in everything from leather and rubber to nylon and chrome. Some also have vibrators to double both of your pleasure. But don't go on a ring-a-ding marathon – these devices should be worn for no longer than 20 minutes max.

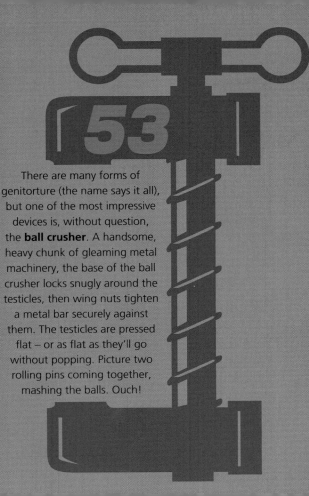

53

There are many forms of genitorture (the name says it all), but one of the most impressive devices is, without question, the **ball crusher**. A handsome, heavy chunk of gleaming metal machinery, the base of the ball crusher locks snugly around the testicles, then wing nuts tighten a metal bar securely against them. The testicles are pressed flat – or as flat as they'll go without popping. Picture two rolling pins coming together, mashing the balls. Ouch!

DEVIOUS
DEVICES

What to get the
serious-minded
S&M aficionado.

- In its simplest form, the **spanking bench** is a wooden sawhorse (with or without a padded top) that the Sub (see Tip 8) can be bent over to get their just rewards. Some are adjustable, which makes it easier to move onto more intimate play once the spanking is done. High-end benches also come with cuffs and vibrators.
- Assume the position and **spreader bars** with cuffs will keep your arms and legs spread wide so that your partner has easy access to your entire body.
- **Suspension bars** are heavy-duty spreader bars that keep you on your toes. You'll need to drill holes in the ceiling to attach them.
- A playground-style **sex swing** with straps will turn your bedroom into a playground. No, this doesn't mean swinging.

HOME HELP

You can break the bank – custom-made, diamond-encrusted snakeskin gag, anyone? – but you don't have to. In fact, you probably have enough double-duty items in your home right now to get together your own carnal torture kit.

55

- For **restraints**, use scarves, neckties, nylons, rope or thick yarn (don't try to undo them afterwards – have scissors nearby to cut your way out).

- Swanky **leashes and dog collars** can be found at your local pet shop – go for the ones with lots of sparkle.

- While you can always use a scarf for a blindfold, a simple **eye mask** from a beauty supply shop will stay in place better.

- Flat-headed **hairbrushes**, slippers or rubber-soled shoes, chopsticks, wooden spoons and rulers will hurt just as good as a specially-made paddle.

- Check out your local DIY store for **heavy-duty hardware** such as ropes, pulleys, hooks and chains.

- Clothes pegs (clothespins) will do in a pinch for **nipple clamps**. Wooden ones are a bit kinder than their plastic cousins. Stretch the metal spring in the clothes peg (clothespin) to make it gentler.

- Break out a **leather belt** as a strap or restraint.

- The best, if ugliest, blindfold/gag/bondage device is probably already stashed somewhere in your bathroom cupboard: an **elastic bandage**.

- Check out *KinkyCrafts: 99 Do-It-Yourself S/M Toys for the Kinky Handyperson* (edited by Lady Green and Jaymes Easton) for instructions on how to make your own **home dungeon** with simple household goods.

KNOW THE ROPES

Here's how to get hog-tied without getting all knotted up.

It can be tricky to tie someone up without making it too tight. A good rule of thumb is to tie loosely with lots of turns of the rope. This way, you can easily make things tighter or looser with a simple twist. Make sure that you can easily fit two fingers between the restraint and your partner's skin and they can wiggle their fingers and/or toes. Always keep scissors handy just in case. Here are three classic knots to put on your belt.

Slipknots can easily be tied and just as easily untied. Grab anywhere along the length of the rope – this divides the rope into 'left' and 'right' parts. Twist the rope forming a loop. The direction doesn't matter. Pick up one of the ends. Whichever side you pick up will be the part that slips. Make a fold in the part you picked up. Stick the fold through the loop. Be sure to stick it through the opposite direction to the one in which the loop went – if the loop had been twisted the other way, you would stick the fold through the loop in the other direction. When you're finished, one part slides and the other doesn't.

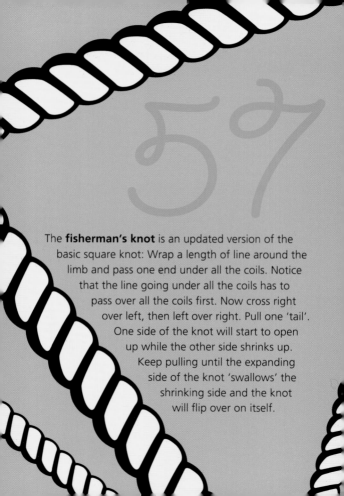

The **fisherman's knot** is an updated version of the basic square knot: Wrap a length of line around the limb and pass one end under all the coils. Notice that the line going under all the coils has to pass over all the coils first. Now cross right over left, then left over right. Pull one 'tail'. One side of the knot will start to open up while the other side shrinks up. Keep pulling until the expanding side of the knot 'swallows' the shrinking side and the knot will flip over on itself.

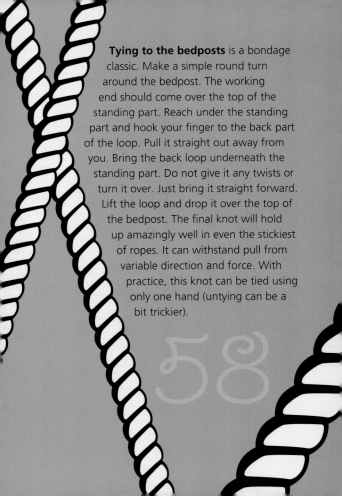

Tying to the bedposts is a bondage classic. Make a simple round turn around the bedpost. The working end should come over the top of the standing part. Reach under the standing part and hook your finger to the back part of the loop. Pull it straight out away from you. Bring the back loop underneath the standing part. Do not give it any twists or turn it over. Just bring it straight forward. Lift the loop and drop it over the top of the bedpost. The final knot will hold up amazingly well in even the stickiest of ropes. It can withstand pull from variable direction and force. With practice, this knot can be tied using only one hand (untying can be a bit trickier).

58

3 POWER PLAYS

The key to any trip into the world of the wild side of sex is figuring out how to push your buttons by pushing your comfort level. For some people, it's about indulging their inner tyrant – telling their lover exactly what to do without ever saying 'please'. For others, the thrill is in lying back and being the centre of someone's erotic attention. And for others, it's a heady combo of both of these pleasures. Read on and choose your position… again and again.

YOUR MISTRESS MANUAL

You get to order him around and have an orgasm. What could be better?

Get **inspiration** on how to work your inner Dom from these **powerful film vixens**:

- Alex Wood in *Fatal Attraction*: Seemingly mild-mannered Alex refuses to take 'no' for an answer.
- Catherine Tramell in *Basic Instinct* and *Basic Instinct 2*: She's a trisexual, hard-living hedonist.
- Franny in *In the Cut*: This emotionally stifled school-teacher by day is a steamy, psycho killer by night.
- Séverine in *Belle du Jour*: Skip the subtitles and watch as the sexy heroine indulges in her S&M fantasies.

Greet him **dressed in black leather** from head-to-toe, stilettos and holding a small paddle or whip. Tell him he has three minutes to get undressed or risk getting punished. Punish him anyway. You choose – you can make him your plaything or order him to ravish you from head to toe.

61

Practise orgasm control – his. Stroke him but **forbid him to climax**. Enjoy taking your time with your willing victim – drive him to distraction and bring him to the edge of ecstasy, then back off and make him plead for more!

Up the **dominatrix** ante – first tell him to do the laundry, cleaning and all of the other household chores. *Then*, stroke him and forbid him to climax. Want to really make him squirm? Tie him up and go to town **pleasuring yourself**. He can't touch until you release him.

62

TO LOVE AND OBEY

Not everyone is looking for a kiss and a cuddle. Sometimes all you want is unadulterated raw sex… with someone else in charge. Here's how to submit instantly – no experience necessary.

You are ordered to immediately purchase a **Sexy Slave Kit** (see Section Two: Toys 'R' Lust). It includes kinky red wrist and ankle cuffs, a soft blindfold and a teasing feather.

Find an outfit that makes you feel the role – a particular pair of boots, a certain lipstick colour, a bustier or a French maid's outfit. Get **dressed up and ready to play**.

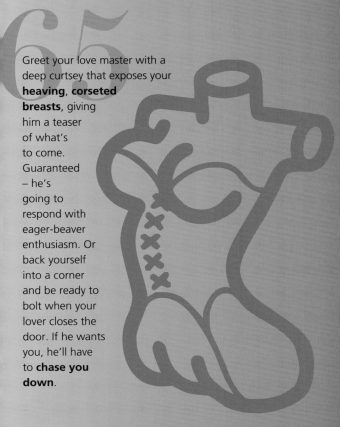

65

Greet your love master with a deep curtsey that exposes your **heaving**, **corseted breasts**, giving him a teaser of what's to come. Guaranteed – he's going to respond with eager-beaver enthusiasm. Or back yourself into a corner and be ready to bolt when your lover closes the door. If he wants you, he'll have to **chase you down**.

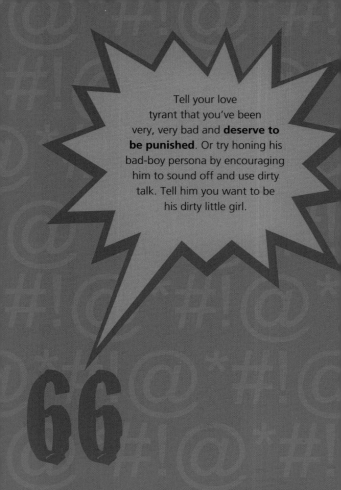

Tell your love tyrant that you've been very, very bad and **deserve to be punished**. Or try honing his bad-boy persona by encouraging him to sound off and use dirty talk. Tell him you want to be his dirty little girl.

66

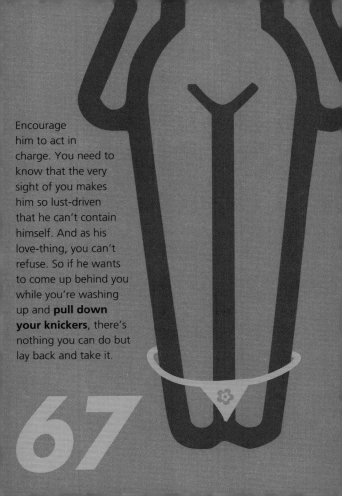

Encourage him to act in charge. You need to know that the very sight of you makes him so lust-driven that he can't contain himself. And as his love-thing, you can't refuse. So if he wants to come up behind you while you're washing up and **pull down your knickers**, there's nothing you can do but lay back and take it.

67

START A SCENE

Here are eight scenes to get the action started. All of these roles are unisex so you can switch parts. One word of caution: avoid characters and scenarios that are complicated, or that you're not familiar or comfortable with, or you'll spend more time on the prep than the play.

Older Lover/Inexperienced Partner: Play an older, experienced lover dominating a shy young playmate, teaching them how to have fun between the sheets.

Employee/Boss: Be the stern boss and teach your employee a lesson in – er – leadership.

68

Stripper/Customer: The stripper can touch the client, but the client can't touch the stripper – except to tip.

Hooker/Client: Go high-class or down-and-dirty. Either way, the hooker does all the work.

Pornstar/Director: Pretend to be working with your favourite star, giving them very precise directions on how to please themselves.

Patient/Doctor: Play the medic who gets seduced by their randy patient. Another take is to be a sex therapist unsuccessfully trying to cure a sex fiend.

Teacher/Student: Your pupil has been very naughty and needs to be punished.

Cop/Thief: You've been very, very bad and the police are going to have to handcuff you and take you in.

4 HURTS SO GOOD

Like any randy wrangling, even a little slap and tickle will get ho-hum if you stick with the same routine every time. Whipping up something new keeps things interesting each and every time. Read on for some no-sweat ways to expand your pain programme. Bring it on!

NO EQUIPMENT NEEDED

You don't have to own a wardrobe of latex or master more than the basics of the lingo to get into the pain game. Here's how to get your freak on without the frills.

A simple **'don't move an inch'** may be the only restraint you need. Mix in some gentle scratching, pinching and a few light bites and you're playing with power.

69

Get things started by lying spread out and **tell your lover to do what they will**. Then spell out the following scenario: he turns you around, holds your wrists behind your back with one hand and wraps his other hand around your hair, lightly pulling it while penetrating you, doggy style. After a few minutes, he withdraws, turns you around, places a hand over your neck and goes back in for more.

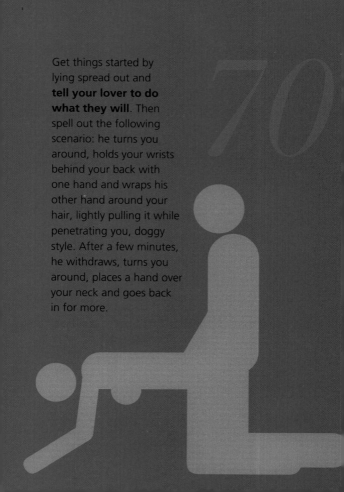

Take turns tying each other up spread-eagled and buzzing various pleasure points with a vibrator. Stop and make them **beg for more**.

72

Order him to take off your high-heeled boots and caress your feet. Then tell him to **take his hands higher**.

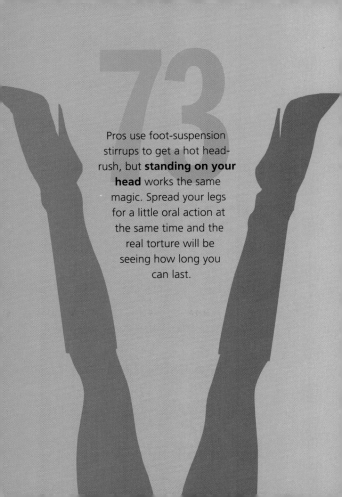

Pros use foot-suspension stirrups to get a hot head-rush, but **standing on your head** works the same magic. Spread your legs for a little oral action at the same time and the real torture will be seeing how long you can last.

FIT TO BE TIED

Show some restraint – no strings attached. Be sure to take your time restraining your lover. Doing it slowly makes the experience more erotic, plus you can make sure you get it right. Here are some sweet ways to get tied up in knots (twist back to Tips 56–58 for more knotty advice).

74

That **classic bondage position** of legs wide open and arms secured got that way mostly because it works. One common mistake is to tie the legs together but that's the wrong kind of torture as he can't gain access.

75

Make like a Buddha with the **Lotus tie**. Fold their legs in a floor-sitting position and wrap the ankles together.

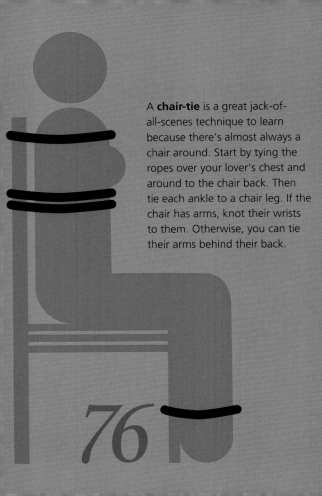

A **chair-tie** is a great jack-of-all-scenes technique to learn because there's almost always a chair around. Start by tying the ropes over your lover's chest and around to the chair back. Then tie each ankle to a chair leg. If the chair has arms, knot their wrists to them. Otherwise, you can tie their arms behind their back.

76

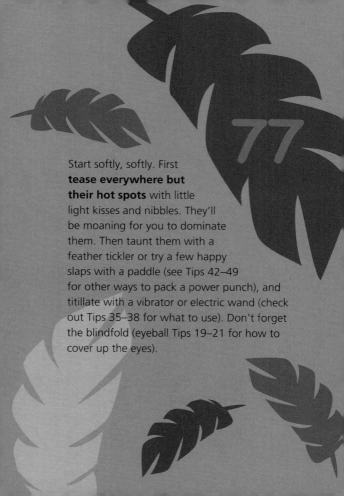

Start softly, softly. First **tease everywhere but their hot spots** with little light kisses and nibbles. They'll be moaning for you to dominate them. Then taunt them with a feather tickler or try a few happy slaps with a paddle (see Tips 42–49 for other ways to pack a power punch), and titillate with a vibrator or electric wand (check out Tips 35–38 for what to use). Don't forget the blindfold (eyeball Tips 19–21 for how to cover up the eyes).

77

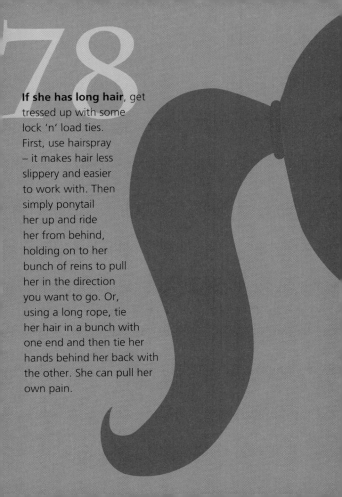

78

If she has long hair, get tressed up with some lock 'n' load ties. First, use hairspray – it makes hair less slippery and easier to work with. Then simply ponytail her up and ride her from behind, holding on to her bunch of reins to pull her in the direction you want to go. Or, using a long rope, tie her hair in a bunch with one end and then tie her hands behind her back with the other. She can pull her own pain.

GET SENSIBLE

Your senses are the way you experience the world. Putting yours in someone else's control is one of the most submissive things you can do.

Love Is Blind

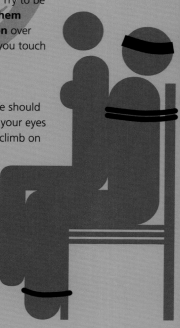

- Cover your lover's eyes. Try to be extra quiet and **make them drool with anticipation** over when, where and how you touch them next.
- Try the tips in this book **blindfolded**.
- Instead of a blindfold, he should come behind and cover your eyes with his **hands**. Or you climb on top and cover his eyes while you bounce up and down.
- Blindfold him and give him a **lap dance**. Up the stakes by tying him to the chair first (see Tip 76 for the perfect technique).

80

Get in Touch

• Alternate **hot and cold sensations** by running ice over your lover's body and then dripping hot wax onto them. Pay special attention to their moan zones.

• Get clipped: check out Tips 50–53 for what **clips or clamps** to use and then Tips 92–94 for what to do.

• There's nothing tinglier for titillating torture than a **tickle** (say that three times quickly!). Try using a feather or your fingers.

• Lubricate the head of a **plunger** and press and release it up and down your bodies. It feels like a giant crushing kiss and the extra juice causes a slight suction before release.

• Give each other a **full-body massage** with some body scrub. Rub as hard as you dare. Or break out loofah mittens and get scratching.

Listen Up

- After you blindfold your partner, keep them even more in the dark with earmuffs to **block out sound.**
- Get in tune with a **torture playlist**. At http://fetishexchange.org/scene-music01.shtml, there are music suggestions to groove to for bondage scenes, whipping and flogging. Get down and shake your booty.

81

Tongue Tasters

- Go classic and re-enact the famous scene from *9½ Weeks*. Then check out the rest of the movie for straight razor on nipple play, hot wax drips and a little **girl-on-girl action**.
- **Take a bite.** Kinsey reported that about half of all men and women are aroused by being nibbled on.

82

Made to Odour

- The reason leather is big in the S&M world is that it smells oh-so-good. Make him come hither by slipping on a **leather glove** and playing with yourself. Once your hand is juiced, use it to gag him.

- Add some real spice to your naughty games – crush some whole peppercorns, wrap them in a white handkerchief and secure it with a rubber band. When you feel your man reaching orgasm, have him hold the pepper hanky under your nose just as your climax is on the horizon. The sneeze you'll have at orgasm will cause your vaginal muscles to clamp down on him inside you and intensify the orgasmic waves. Meanwhile, when he has the **pepper hanky**, the force of his ejaculation will be intensified as he shoots in tandem with the force of his sneeze.

83

WHAT A SPANKER

Up for some playful paddling? Here are a few sizzling ways to have a spanking good time.

84

However you **sock it to 'em** – hand, paddle, hairbrush – start off striking lightly, then gradually make the beat more intense. If you hit too strong too soon and too quickly, you will hurt your lover in a definitely not sexy way.

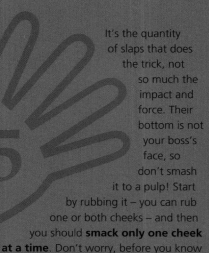

It's the quantity of slaps that does the trick, not so much the impact and force. Their bottom is not your boss's face, so don't smash it to a pulp! Start by rubbing it – you can rub one or both cheeks – and then you should **smack only one cheek at a time**. Don't worry, before you know it, they'll turn the other cheek...

The key to making your smackdown blissful is **location**, **location**, **location** (study Tip 12 so you know where never to hit). Hit the bull's-eye by aiming where the butt cheek meets the thigh, or spread the buns and softly spank the anal area with two or three fingers. Spanking close to the genitals will also send the receiver into sweet oblivion.

The further your hips are bent, the stronger the impact. So it's better to **strike a pose** over on your hands and knees, over your lover's lap, the kitchen table, or the bonnet (hood) of your car – use your imagination. The classic pose lets you brace yourself against their blows while simultaneously exposing your rear for a good licking.

87

To intensify things, don't hit harder. Instead, relax your wrist. If you're using your hand, **alternate** between spreading your fingers to widen the stingy effect and cupping your hands to smooth things over. Take a breather after each smack to let the sensation sink in. Mix the moment up with a bottom rub before resuming. For a **wildly wanton whack**, spank with a leather-gloved hand.

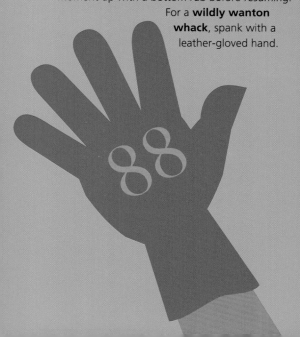

88

89

Work some light stroking, scratching and rubbing into your spanking. Don't forget to **rub-a-dub-dub** their other bits and pieces at the same time to keep things painfully fabulous. If you're using a hairbrush, switch things around and apply the bristle side every few smacks.

Good spankers have **good rhythm**. The winning beat is: two light smacks, one slightly harder, then three light smacks and one hard one, and repeat. This build-up will deem you master.

Role with it:
Spanking and
fantasy are the
dynamic duo of
the S&M scene.
Experienced spankers
concentrate on the
mental foreplay first by
announcing the 'punishment'
and ordering their 'badly
behaved' partner to stand in the
corner and **wait for punishment**.
Favourite plays include daddy or
uncle and naughty girl, teacher
and badly behaved student, and
so on (see Tip 68 for favourite
characters). **End with
a bang** – the receiver
promises to mend their
ways and shows just how
good they can be.

91

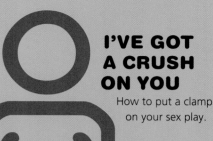

I'VE GOT A CRUSH ON YOU

How to put a clamp on your sex play.

Don't put the pinch on your lover until they are turned on and always **apply it to the tip of their bits**. Parts of the body worth pinching are the belly button, inner thigh or arm, vaginal lips, fingers and toes, earlobes and nipples. Try clipping both nipples, then connect them with a chain and gently pull.

92

93

Remove clips or clamps after 30 minutes to **avoid unnecessary pain**. The area will still tingle for a few hours, so take advantage of the extra sensitivity by alternating between lightly paddling and tickling the skin.

94

Brush against the clip or clamp or **tug at it gently** to increase the sensation.

GET WHIPPED INTO SHAPE

If you've ever spanked anyone for a long time, you know that your spanking hand wears out quickly! Well, that's what whips are for. Here's how to give different strokes for different folks.

95

It's all in the aim. First-timers should practise their technique on a pillow (and swot up on Tip 13). Shoot for a **caressing flick** rather than a stinging blow.

96

Take it bent over or lying face down. Flogging someone who is standing unsupported can knock them down. **Gently drag the striker** over the skin, letting the person get a feel for the instrument and excited about what's coming.

Time yourself. Go for a **strike-rest-strike rhythm** of around one stroke every few seconds to give the person on the receiving end time to register the blow and anticipate the next one.

Have a few **different strikers** in your arsenal so that you can play with sensations (see Tips 42–49 for everything whip). Then you can move from stinging light switches to biting canes, to soft fleeces to a quick tickle and back again.

BALL BUSTERS

His boys are tougher than you think. Here's how to have a balls-up with the family jewels.

99

Give his ball-cock a yank with a light slapping, stiletto prod or even a few flogs. The blood rush will give him an explosive orgasm – but make sure you avoid the underside as you can cause damage to the urethra.

Pin the tail on his donkey – you'll be amazed at how many clips and clamps you can get on his penis and balls, especially if he's uncut. He'll love the stinging sensation.

101

Smear some spearmint or peppermint oil over his penis or scrotum for an **all-over fresh tingle**. Or 'paint' melted wax on his brush and peel it off.

102

Catch and release his balls by binding them with a stocking or testicle cuffs and pulling tight before letting go. The tight and loose sensation will have him wriggling on your hook.

103

Make him melt by inserting an ice cube into the end of a condom and then suiting him up.

104

Wrap a silk scarf or stocking around his wood and **'shine' it** (like you would a shoe). He'll sparkle with pleasure.

Tie his jewels up with leather strips, ribbons or velvet cords. Be as ornamental as you please – tying up an erect cock can create a luscious work of art, and teasing it can be even more artistic, while a few slaps are extra exciting.

Barra, Vatersay, Sandray and Pabbay

Macc and Other Islands

Graham Wilson

MACC AND OTHER ISLANDS

illustrated by Gerry Dale

Millrace

First published in Great Britain in 2004 by
Millrace
2a Leafield Road, Disley
Cheshire SK12 2JF

Text © 2004 Graham Wilson
Illustrations © 2004 Gerry Dale

ISBN: 1 902173 155

Typeset in Berthold Baskerville.
Manufactured in the United Kingdom
by LPPS Ltd, Wellingborough, Northants NN8 3PJ

Acknowledgements

The most obvious debt that I have to acknowledge is to all those who have written on this subject before me. The bibliography indicates the extent of my plundering. Its contents, however, are much more than various points of reference and I would commend each of the books to any reader who is attracted to the particular combination of mountains and sea.

Of them all, *The Scottish Islands* by Hamish Haswell-Smith has been the most useful. This handsome volume details all the Scottish islands that lie within the author's definition. These number 165 and the book contains a wealth of detail on the history, wildlife and physical features of each one. It is aimed, primarily, at those who hope to arrive under their own steam (or sail), which is probably the ideal way to make such a journey.

But I suppose my greatest debt is to the Ordnance Survey and the maps it produces of the more obscure parts of Britain – *Explorer* 460 was particularly helpful. As the majority of the 'other islands' are in Scotland, much of the nomenclature is in Gaelic. It is, therefore, wise for the hillwalker to acquire a smattering of the relevant terms. Particularly if the *Sron* (ridge) that you have blithely bisected with your latest compass bearing is described both as *Cas* (steep) and *Mhor* (big) and turns out to be a cliff. To this end, I would direct the prudent towards the appendix on Mountaineering Gaelic to be found in Hamish Brown's account of his journey around the Munros in *Hamish's Mountain Walk.*

I would also like to thank Roger Newton, a former Classics teacher at The King's School in Macclesfield, for his elegant translation of Haskett Smith's outburst on page 74. His rendering reflects Homer's skill in making the movement of the verse complement the sense of the words.

Finally, my thanks to my family and, particularly, the younger members who, for many years, were brainwashed into believing that getting cold and wet was a necessary part of any summer holiday. At least, until that fateful day in the Youth Hostel at Crianlarich when they discovered a discarded travel brochure on island holidays in the Med.

GPW

Contents

A Preface

Well, *for a start, you'll have to explain to them why you think it is.*

The *them* was any potential purchaser of the book that you now hold in your hand and *it* was Macc (aka Macclesfield) and the sentence as a whole was an answer to the question that I had just asked. Perhaps it would be better if I start at the beginning.

Six years ago, I had written another 'Macc &' book and my current drinking companion had complained that he had been misled. He had assumed the 'Art of Long Distance Walking' indicated some self-help volume that, in a Zen-like manner, allowed the enlightened to travel vast distances without actually going to the trouble of getting out of bed. Instead, he had found that it was little more than a series of tedious trudges around what appeared to be the Gobi Desert. (It might be pertinent at this point to mention that my companion's idea of a desert is where the traveller has to move more than seventy-five yards to the next watering-hole.)

So, on this occasion, I decided it wiser to consult the oracle on the likelihood of an offence against the Trades Description Act before, rather than after, publication. Readers are rather like Mr Worthing's parents – to lose one might be regarded as a misfortune but further carelessness might bring the full weight of a Publishing House down around my ears. To pre-empt this possibility, I had floated the title before him and asked his opinion. As a result, I had to accept the consequences of the opportunity offered.

As I see it (pause to allow the attentive to anticipate the pun; Half a Lager Joe looked up) *for Macc to be an island, it has to be entirely surrounded by water or, as I see it, sea. And as the town* (an attempt to download into his mind a map of Cheshire and environ) *must be at least fifty miles, as the cat swings, from the saline solution, Macc can hardly be said to be surrounded by water.*

I was beginning to regret my decision but, looking through the window at the streets awash with the latest torrential storm, decided it was better to accept the pouring within which was now in full stream.

So the key to the situation is that, before you start opening another Pandora's box of All Our Yesterdays, you should at least attempt to justify the statement. I know you had a half-hearted stab at it in that other Macc thing, but you'll have to do rather better than the Setting-Up-Camp-on-a-Breeze-Block-in-the-Middle-of-the-Bollin mullarky. And that poet fella, didn't he say, 'No man is an island', or words to that effect, and probably, if pushed, would apply the same principle to most other things. (short hiatus) *Other, of course, than islands.*

He paused and looked to his fellow audience, confident that the neat and circular nature of his argument would gain their approval. Half a Lager Joe quivered. But then another idea seemed to strike.

But does that mean, and I leave you with this final thought, that neither the Isle of Man nor — with a slight lowering of the head to allow a conspiratorial glance over the top of his glasses — *the Isle of Wight can properly deserve the epithet of 'insular'?*

With that, he drained his glass and, to the chagrin of certain parties, departed. But not without a Parthian shot.

And while you're about it, you may as well explain exactly what you mean by 'other'.

As there is no point in asking advice and consistently ignoring it, or backing a dog and barking yourself, as the pundits have it, I will try to explain why I think Macc is an island.

3

Geophysically, the centre of the town lies in a basin perched halfway up a hill, which means that when it snows it is quickly surrounded by water, albeit solid, leaving the inhabitants marooned for days or even, at one time, weeks. Thus, cut off from civilisation as they knew it, they were quick to adopt the islander's curiosity about events in the outside world. This may well account for the town's universal and enthusiastic public greeting of 'wha'dya know', as if the enquirer at last had an opportunity for an update on the siege of Mafeking or the state of Queen Anne's health. Once the snows melt, the island quickly reverts to a plug hole, as such nomenclature as Waters Green and The Dams suggest.

Metaphysically also, (to take up the cudgels against the former Dean of St Paul's), Macc is an island or rather, for a portion of its inhabitants, an archipelago. The town was famous for its silk and as a result the principal workforce consisted of women who 'with their nimbler fingers and less demanding wage structures, proved irresistible to accountants and employers alike'. The men were left to drift across the uncertain seas of part-time jobs and racing tips. Clearly such a voyage required the occasional landfall and this was provided by a plethora

4

of public houses. Although the present gaggle is only a shadow of its former self, and now so many lie undone, overtaken by the tidal wave of Ladies' Hairdressers and Mobile Phone Emporiums, it has still sufficient in number to merit a collective noun. At least sufficient to provide a rock to which a drowning man might cling.

Here may still be found the once ubiquitous Jobbing Builder, a Crusoe waiting for Friday. Having no official office of work other than a plastic bag of dismembered cigarette packets covered by a variety of figures, he was inevitably drawn to the epicentre of the casual labour market. And for him it was a comfortable milieu. He knew where he stood and it didn't really matter which one he stood in – they were much of a muchness. In fact, a theory was once posited that such was the sameness that it was not impossible, as some offshoot of Einstein's greater principle, that in the space–time continuum that is Macc, the members of the drinking population stood still and at relative intervals the pubs moved around them.

Another common factor was that, as all the women were at work, the daytime clientele was exclusively male, which tended to reinforce the insular nature of things. On one occasion, the most revered of these sceptred isles was overtaken by a flurry of chiffon and challenging *chapeaux*. This group of young ladies had been disgorged from a nearby wedding and were in search of refreshment and whatever amusement the premises might afford. No doubt in their natural southern climes this would be regarded as an unexceptional course of action. But not in Macc. To this day the elders still retell the tale and, for many years after, the sight of an unfamiliar headpiece silhouetted against the frosted glass panel of the taproom door caused the same level of panic as once did the sails of Viking longships.

Despite Donne's protestation, I feel that man, or a particular type of man, can also be seen as an island. The individual who has deliberately severed connections with the mainland of conventional behaviour and steers a self-reliant course could be described in this way. The sort who would accept a free drink, but never ask for one. A generation ago, such characters abounded and Macc was not short of its share. The nanny state has long swept most such beneath its skirts but one survived into the twenty-first century.

He had spent the best part of his life living in Macclesfield Forest, fending for himself in the manner of his forebears, but eventually a combination of arthritis and the caring community caught up with him. The well-wishers provided a sheltered home and an electric wheelchair. He was quite happy with this arrangement. The former provided excellent storage space for all the bits and pieces (usually scrap metal) that he had 'dropped on' and the latter an inexpensive form of transport to the pub. More importantly, it also ensured a secure passage home. To offset any deviance that his lunchtime indulgence might have caused, he determinedly straddled a white line that the local authority had so thoughtfully placed down the middle of the road. It was an interesting sight to watch a caravan of juggernauts proceeding in a stately fashion along the main road to Chester, led by the diminutive form of a man with long grey hair, peering bleary-eyed over the handlebars of his motorised tricycle.

As for the 'other' in the title, the pages that follow describe a variety of the conventional sort. I feel, however, that these islands are but an example of eccentricity of all kinds and that the term should not be limited to the dictionary definition of a piece of land surrounded by water. There are people, places and memories we isolate in our minds in a particular way or for a particular reason. For my part, they seem to be often associated with high places. Over the years, mountains have been seen as islands within islands, surrounded by seas of myth and tales of their invincibility. To the Munroist, the Inaccessible Pinnacle of Sgurr Dearg is more isolated than its parent isle and if I were to try to persuade the most sceptical to my point of view, I would attempt to summon up the vision where the valleys are in a low-slung cloud from which a reef of sunlit summits springs.

However, I may as well have saved myself the bother. Just when I had sorted in my own mind which, what or even who is an island, the EU pronounced. In the lead-up to the reorganisation of Europe in 2006, it has decided that an island is not an island if it has fewer than 50 residents, is attached to the mainland by a rigid structure, is less than 1 km from the mainland, or is home to the capital of an EU state. Thus, at a stroke, the majority of the British Isles will cease to be, including the largest and most misty of them all. I assume the motive is to cut back on the amount of insular aid that the Union is legally obliged to provide and that when it comes to doling out care in this particular community, Skye's the limit.

This Island Race

It must have been in some moment of middish-life crisis that I announced that I wanted 'to chuck it all in and take up crofting in the Outer Hebrides'. This outburst appeared to cause the usual level of anxiety on the domestic front, i.e. polite indifference. Except that, a few weeks later, a cutting advertising a family holiday at the Castlebay Hotel on the Hebridean island of Barra was presented at the breakfast table. As this seemed a suitable compromise between striking a Thoreauvian pose and fulfilling familial duties, the appropriate letter was despatched.

All this happened in January and as the Odyssey was not due to set sail until August, the matter, for the most part, slipped my mind. It was only when people enquired about my holiday plans that curiosity returned. Having delivered the information that Barra was my destination, I noticed, not the expected response congratulating my enterprising spirit, but the look usually reserved for the unfortunate error of judgement made by an ingenuous child. It was only on much later consideration that I realised they had thought my resort of choice was a shipbuilding town on the southern coast of Cumbria.

Time passed and it began to dawn on me that my package holiday would probably not include a posse of couriers brandishing placards or brightly-coloured umbrellas. It was up to me to sort out the travel arrangements. I discovered that a boat left Oban for Castlebay mid-afternoon on the appropriate day and that there were trains from Macclesfield to this point of departure via various Glasgow railway stations. My AA *Road Book of Scotland* (pub. 1953) showed that there was a road on the island but as Kelloggs were offering (provided you devoured enough cornflakes) free rail travel for spouse and off-spring, public transport seemed more attractive than the heavily-priced car ferry.

The crossing was for the most part uneventful. The weather was good, with the hills of Mull basking in the sunlight, and I looked upon these and my efforts with a sense of satisfaction. I am not sure I realised which hill was which and certainly it never crossed my mind that the same family group would many years later stand on the highest to celebrate my final Munro. In fact, I don't think I knew a

Munro from a Murdoch at the time. We stopped in the Sound of Mull opposite Tobermory to collect a vehicle. A tender drew up alongside. A panel slid open amidships and a lorry clambered aboard as though involved in some reverse caesarean section. Coll and Tiree were left astern. Then nothing. The satisfactory sense began to be replaced by a feeling of slight unease and in trying to fathom the cause I realised that I had never been at sea before. I had been on the sea – Channel crossings, pleasure trips across Morecambe Bay, etc – but never at sea. It's a bit like your first white-out. The compass says where you want to go is where it's pointing, but there's always that niggle of doubt.

Eventually land appeared, at first imperceptibly but then in the sudden rush that always precedes a passing into harbour. There are times in life when the first glimpse of a view overtakes you – the initial bump into the Buachaille, as the herdsman presides over the impending gloom of Glencoe, mounting the slopes of Glen Desssarry onto the ridge of Sgurr na Ciche, when a panorama of lochs, islands and hills bursts like a firework display out of the drear heather slopes of your ascent, turning the corner into Kinloch Hourn to see the last of the sun set alight the sails of a three-masted schooner, a latter-day Téméraire. These are the things you remember and store against the dismal plod up the unforgiving Meallach that has sufficiently withstood the elements to keep its head above the Munro Plimsoll line.

Such a view was the first sight of Barra. The evening sunshine fell obliquely across the harbour, sharpening the edges of Kisimul Castle, the water-bound fastness of the MacNeils, former Lords of the Isles. As the boat approached the quay, the eye followed the rise of tiered buildings caught in the arms of the land that formed the bay. Small windows catching the sun were dominated by the hotel and church. But this architecture to God and Mammon is completely upstaged by the hill of Heaval that seems to overwhelm the backdrop and lord it over the mortals who have pinched a grip on this isolated spot.

But there is something more than the view that catches the eye. I couldn't work out what it was at first. Then I realised it was the crowd on the quay-side. They were not waiting to embark but to welcome. Eyes on the pier searched for familiar faces as generations before them must have waited, in half hope half fear, for the return of the herring fleet with sustenance, family and friends. At a time when most of the mainland is shut, Castlebay had sprung to life. The shop was open, the Information Centre poised to give advice, the public bar of the Castlebay Hotel braced for the inevitable onslaught of reunion and general rejoicing.

I quickly realised that the locals have a different slant on life from Macclesfield Man. An early example was when I tried to glean some local knowledge from the elders at the bar. This was a family holiday. Hence visits to the beach were a prerequisite. There are many fine stretches of sand on the west coast but quite a long walk for small legs. I had spotted on my OS map (Second Series: Sheet 31) a small cove just round the headland from the village. My concern, as it lay near the narrows of the Sound dividing Barra from its neighbour Vatersay, was whether bathing might be dangerous. So, unfolding the map, I made the necessary enquiries. A discussion followed, for the most part in English (I assumed for my benefit) but highlighted with chippings of Gaelic when (again I assumed) precision was required. I began to realise that it was not my question that had caused such animation but the map itself, which they were orientating on the bar counter with intermittent finger-jabbing. Eventually, with much shaking of heads, the map was neatly refolded and returned. I repeated my question but this produced only non-committal replies. Comprehension dawned. Although it was all very interesting to look at a picture of their island and even see the names of their homes in print, as a source for informed navigation it was completely useless. If I really wanted to find my way about, what I needed was a chart.

The other misunderstanding was more serious. On my travels around the island I had noticed a number of houses and cottages that appeared to be empty. Emboldened by the welcome I had received and, no doubt, the whisky chasers that are handed around the company as other cultures proffer cigarettes, I asked if any of the empty properties were for sale. I have often wondered, after the event, if I could have done anything to have given greater offence. The group, not ostentatiously but nevertheless deliberately, dispersed until I found myself standing alone, save for the barman who had little alternative but to stop. He carefully, if not over meticulously, washed and dried the glasses of the too dearly departed, before offering the following piece of advice: *There are no empty houses on Barra, just those waiting for the people to return.*

Duly chastened, I beat the due retreat. Fortunately, there was no long-term damage. The rest of the family had made a sufficiently sound impression for my behaviour to be put down to ignorance rather than arrogance.

And that was a fair assessment. I had no real grasp of the way that the ruling classes (let it be made clear at this point, not exclusively English) had strangled the Highlands and Islands by clearing out the people to maximise the space for breeding sheep. How this all came about is a complicated story, often given to partial oversimplification, but at the heart of it was the movement from the concept of a clan, where the chieftain held the land in trust for his followers (clan is the Gaelic for child), to that of the laird who, as self-proclaimed owner, cashed in on the old feudal loyalties and absented himself for pastures new. He left in his place a factor whose job was to extort as much from the land as possible to match his employer's indulgence in the fleshpots of the south. When the money ran out, he simply sold what had been everyman's land, now masquerading as an estate, with all the pseudo-legal implications of such a term, to the highest bidder. Such purchasers often neither knew nor cared about the culture they had stumbled across and, regardless of suffering, exploited the situation as they thought suited them best.

Barra was no exception. It was bought for £38,050 in 1858 by Colonel John Gordon, who attempted to sell it to the British government as a convict station. Her Majesty declined but in some deal or other offered the Colonel a grant to transport the inhabitants of the island to the east coast of Canada, where they were left to starve. Those who were sufficiently resourceful to escape this nineteenth-century holocaust were hunted down by police and press gangs under the savage direction of the Reverend Henry Beatson. The scenes, according to a eye-witness, were similar to a slave hunt on the African coast. As Beatson was a Presbyterian minister on a predominantly Catholic island, it was not the first time and certainly not the last that religion and economics have joined forces for their mutual benefit. At the time I knew nothing of this. Although I had studied British History throughout the whole of my school career, I had never once heard of the Clearances. The textbooks on which I had been nurtured made no mention. Churchill's *A History of the English Speaking People* made much of the valiant imperial expansion but an inspection of the index of the relevant volume shows no reference to the Highlands in the nineteenth century, let alone the atrocities that occurred. Perhaps the clue is in the title.

In retrospect, the reaction to my insensitivity to local custom could have been worse. Some years previously, I was told, mainland bureaucracy had decided that certain buildings which offered accommodation had to comply with various Health and Safety Regulations. An Inspector was duly despatched, who decided for reasons best known to himself to arrive incognito and put up as a guest in the hotel. He was treated with the usual courtesy and friendship that all visitors are accorded and his habit of wandering around and weighing things up was put down to some unfortunate eccentricity. Eventually he revealed his true colours and rather loftily announced that until certain alterations had been made the premises could well be shut until further notice. The reaction of the Public Bar, on hearing about this London-inspired fatwa, was to frogmarch the perpetrator down to the harbour and throw him off the end of the pier.

Whether the story is apocryphal or merely embroidered, I have no idea, but it is certainly consistent with the islanders' way of thinking. To abuse their hospitality was inexcusable and for a off-comer to have the effrontery to tell them how they should order their complex and, at times, fragile socio-economic structure was, to say the least, presumptuous.

Discovering the island as a place is not so complex and the best way to start is from the top of Heaval, the highest point available. Though only 1255 feet high, it features in the SMC *Hillwalkers' Guide to the Corbetts and Other Scottish Hills* and rightly so, for it is a grand little peak that does not have to be propped up by statistics. From the summit you can see the whole geography laid out before you like the map you hold in your hand or – as you will discover – almost the whole of it. The island is roughly diamond-shaped, with bits sticking out. It has been likened with some justification to a malformed turtle with a leg/flipper in each corner and a neck-like peninsular at the top or north end. This last appendage, springing from the other natural harbour of North Bay, is an intriguing piece of land. At its narrowest, it is less than half a mile across and bounded by two bands of sand. To the west Traigh Eais, to the east Traigh Mhor and, where it broadens into the head, it holds the township of Eoligarry which contains, in turn, corncrakes and the mortal remains of Compton Mackenzie.

Traigh Eais must be one of the best beaches in the world. It is a mile long, with sand that has been beaten into a silver fineness by the umpteenity of Atlantic breakers, sheltered by dunes to the rear and enclosed on each side by a cascade of rock pools as the bay curves against the full force of the ocean's onslaught. On our first visit we had the whole stretch to ourselves for several hours. Eventually another party set up camp some several hundred yards away. The day in question was Bank Holiday Monday. Although I am a man who has openly despised the idea of wasting precious holiday time lazing around on a beach, I couldn't imagine visiting Barra and not spending at least part of a day on Traigh Eais.

Its opposite number, Traigh Mhor, is known also as the Cockle Strand and has a number of interesting features. Not only do its shellfish provide a substantial supplement to the local economy, but at low tide the firm sand is the island's airport. British Airways Express (formerly Loganair) runs a daily service from Glasgow, possibly the only regular service in the world where the flight schedule is governed by the times of the tide. A running battle is in progress as to whether this should be replaced by a hard strip built on the sand and surrounding croft land and protected by a sea wall. The argument in favour is that it would produce a more frequent and reliable service and allow the use of larger aircraft, which in turn would bring in more tourists.

However, an attempt to replace the Twin Otter with the Shorts 360 has so far proved anything but successful. Unlike the Otter, which can operate in a low cloud base and difficult crosswinds, the 360 lived up to its name and fell short all too often. Flights were regularly cancelled and Loganair was forced to return to the original model. In addition, there are serious objections to the scheme in principle. Geomorphological studies have shown that the necessary sea wall would all but close the channel between Barra and the off-shore island of Orosay, which in turn would alter the tide patterns. Damage to the cockle beds and potential flooding of nearby land and property is a likely outcome. The problem will have to be resolved as the Twin Otter is running out of spares. Selfishly, I hope the surrounding waters are too deep to build a bridge.

The east and west coasts are as you would expect. Clusters of rocky inlets form the first, curving bays the second. All look worthy of exploration, but it is the view to the south that catches the eye. The slopes of Heaval tumble down to Castlebay, across the harbour to neighbouring Vatersay, then onto the archipelago of islands that peter to the point where Scotland runs out. The names – Sandray, Pabbay, Mingulay, Berneray – trip off the tongue, spilling headlong to the fullstop that is the lighthouse at Barra Head. For many, that steadfast beam must have been the last sight that the forced emigrants had of their beleaguered country.

But in the midst of this euphonic sweep lies a glottal stop: Kisimul Castle, foursquare in the bay itself. Like many of its kind, it had gone to ruin, the stone pillaged for building elsewhere and, under Gordon of Cluny, reduced to the indignity of a her-ring-curing station. But in 1915 a Canadian, Robert Lister, successfully contested his right to be the chief of the MacNeil clan and claimed the castle and most of Barra as his own. He was also an architect and he and his son Ian MacNeil restored the castle to somewhere near its original state. In fact it is more a recreation than a restoration but is sufficient in these Disneyfied days to act as a lodestone to the clan or, rather, the diaspora thereof.

This transatlantic take-over did not sit happily with Compton Mackenzie, who saw himself as the *de facto* lord of the isle. During the Second World War, the MacNeils suggested that 500 children should be evacuated from Glasgow to Barra, a sort of Clearance in reverse, which Sir C Mac K rebuffed in no uncertain proprietorial terms. It may have been that the new owners, having studied the behaviour of their ancestors, were trying in some way to make amends. The last ruling MacNeil, for example, was scarcely a role model for philanthropists. In 1825, from the comfort of his London home, he wrote to the island priest ordering him to harangue his flock from the pulpit on their indolence, finishing with the threat that

> *if I don't on my arrival find them heart and hand engaged in fishing, they shall tramp and the Land shall be this ensuing spring occupied by strangers.*
> (Cooper, 1985)

But back to the view. Thus far, all is clearly seen except the south-west corner, hidden by the bulk of Ben Tangaval. This requires firsthand investigation. In all the mind-maps spawned by *Treasure Island* that have fed the imagination of the young, there has been a bit that is left to the readers' invention, a secret harbour or a smugglers' cave. This surprise discovery of a new land gives an added dollop of satisfaction. It is also true for the adult explorer that progress is more rewarding if you stumble upon something unexpected and previously invisible. The coastline of Doirlinn Head does not disappoint.

From the summit of the Ben, descend due west until a small hanging valley named as Glen Bretadale on the 1:25000 map leads to a ravine falling towards the sea. There are probably no dragons but on my first visit I was startled enough by the sudden appearance of a disturbed peregrine swooping up the cleft. The walls narrow until a vertical rock-step allows access into a cove based on a broad rock platform. From here can be seen the ever-steepening cliffs and natural arch of Doirlinn Head, a view only otherwise available from a boat off the coast. My visits have always deliberately coincided with dry, calm days and if the small or nervous are involved in the party, it would be wise to carry a rope and the odd sling.

There is no such problem in discovering the rest of the island and there is a good circular walk that covers most of the ground. You can, by definition, begin anywhere, but for the sake of ease I will assume the start and finish to be the public bar of the Castlebay Hotel. Skirt Bagh Beag and mount the slopes of Ben Tangaval. Descend as in the previous paragraph until the cliff tops are reached. Continue in a generally northerly direction. I say generally: as anyone who has followed a coastline knows, you are as often going sideways as forwards. This is the most spectacular part of the day. Peering into coves which the path precariously contours allows glimpses of the nesting colonies of kittiwakes and guillemots. Out to sea, gannets, an endless stream of commuters from the breeding grounds of St Kilda and the other Atlantic outliers, perform their acts of apparent kamikaze. From time to time, basking sharks, seriously big, hump the surface. It is tempting to abandon the walk and just sit and watch.

But if you are to make the Isle of Barra Hotel for an early lunch, you must descend to Halaman Bay and cross the sands to that objective. This was another bright idea to attract the tourists. The perpetrators must have made the decision on a fine day and, indeed, on such it is a wonderful location, but they might have considered why the majority of the population have decided to live as far away as possible from the spot. It has not been a success. It is not as though no one tried: the main building is filled with the obligatory tartan drapes and Skyeboatson-gery. But, for much of the time, the picture windows designed to show off the silver sands and westering sun remain opaque with sea-spray. There is, of course, the inevitable public bar with its crossed dirks sinister on a field of sporrans and posters advertising the appearance of a tribute group to Wee Willie Harris, but it is soulless compared to the others on the island. Even the least discerning American visitor, weaned on a diet of Walt-schmaltz, might doubt that this is the true Highland experience as promised in the brochure.

Still, it is a stopping point of sorts and a place to study the map before assaying the ridge of high ground that splits the island. The simplest way forward is to take the road to Borve, then follow the Duarry Burn to the Beul a' Bhealich. A better scheme is to continue on the coast road and where it branches to Craigston take to the slopes of Beinn Mhartainn and, from its summit, head towards the pass via the chambered cairn of Dun Bharpa and Grianan. From here the Completionist will turn north for a there-and-back to Ben Verrisey. Those with an inbuilt compass will swing south over Hartaval to Heaval itself.

Even if you have visited the summit before, there is always, as with a good book or piece of music, something new to appreciate. Though the topography is static, the weather seldom is and there is often the chance of rainbows over Eriskay or indigo storm clouds gathering in the west to engage your attention. If you have timed it right, you might see the afternoon plane lifting off, at first a slightly clumsy toy banking away from the airstrip and then a resolute bird bound on some instinctive flightpath. So, similarly, you turn and direct your step towards the amber liquid of your choice.

Of course, there is much more to Barra. You have only glimpsed the remoter rocky headlands of the east coast that shelter the basking seals. There are the various harbours to be investigated, where such remaining fish as the seals disdain can be purchased directly from the quayside. It is, however, not the creatures of the sea but human greed that has destroyed the stock and the island's staple trade. The locals will tell you – and there are photographs to prove it – that there was a time when the fishing boats moored at Castlebay were so numerous that a man could walk from deck to deck across the Sound to the neighbouring island of Vatersay. There were as many seals then.

Those days are over as, in the end, will be your stay, leaving this island race to its own devices. For me, Barra has always been like a child-remembered holiday – a sense of timelessness that ends, as it began, with a sudden rush. That frantic last-minute packing and tidying of a borrowed house as The Lord of the Isles, previously hidden from view by outlying islands, steams into the bay with purposeful ease before performing a graceful shimmy against the quay.

Eriskay

Eriskay

If Joyce's pier saw itself as a disappointed bridge, then a particular promontory outside the township of Haun must have felt it had achieved the ultimate apotheosis when someone decided to link that part of Eriskay to the mainland of Uist with a causeway. But was this decision really a call for celebration? It meant that Eriskay would be no longer an island, but a suburb of Lochboisdale. Of course, as with all suburbs, such a situation has its advantages. The amenities of South, not to mention North Uist and the intervening Benbecula, would become available by road and the darts and domino teams from The Politician would no longer have to plan their away matches around the vicissitudes of time and tide. No more could the great masters of golf excuse their absence from the Eriskay Open on the grounds that they couldn't get their head round the conjunction of ferry and tee times. The locals, with some justification, must have felt the whole procedure was long overdue and that they, like the rest of Britain, were entitled to move into the eighteenth century, or whenever the system of turnpikes was invented.

But is it all beer and skittles? Was it wise to abandon islandhood so lightly? It was as an island that Eriskay laid claim to its universal notoriety. The renowned breed of Eriskay pony would never have maintained its singularity if the odd Uist stallion had been able to get over the wall. Bonnie Prince Charlie would probably have chosen a different venue for his secret landing from France if the place was likely to be teeming with tourists from the fleshpots of Lochmaddy. And those who selflessly rescued a considerable amount of whisky might not have been given the time that they used so profitably had the authorities been able to proceed at will with lights flashing and sirens screeching. In fact, if the Sound of Eriskay had already been blocked with lumps of rock and concrete, the inspirited SS Politician would not have travelled that way at all.

As any mystery becomes more accessible, then so does the truth. The ponies may not be a rare breed after all – they were not specifically mentioned in a definitive book on the subject. The Young Pretender, the People's Prince, probably didn't share a meal of roasted shellfish with a group of old crones on the beach but, in all likelihood, was immediately whisked off to the best quarters available. Even the whisky mightn't be seen as quite so galore if an up-to-date study of the official records produces a more prosaic account of the struggle between conscience and greed than when it was left to the creative imagination of the myth-makers.

The filming of the fictional version of the last event took place in Barra and is still sufficiently popular to be projected as flickering wallpaper in the bar of the Castlebay Hotel. The book was written during the Second World War and the film followed soon after. There can be no doubt that the audience of the time related their recent wartime experience to the somewhat sentimental version of life that this art portrayed. Britain with its U-boat blockade and a fearsome blitz from the air had been as much beleaguered as any storm-ridden Hebridean island and even the most landlocked middle of Middle England had felt, and could still feel, the reality of Gaunt's dying speech in *Richard II*. The inhabitants of the 'scept'red isle' had embraced the role of defending a 'fortress built by Nature for herself/Against infection and the hand of war'.

Nor was *Whisky Galore* alone in quarrying the

national mood. The delight in putting one over the unsympathetic and bureaucratic official, conveniently transfused into head-shaven Teutonic stupidity, was a stock in trade. Films like *Passport to Pimlico* continued the trait. Here, a London borough discovers that it, through a freak of historical horse-trading, is a country in its own right and not subject to the rule of British law. This story displays a similar sense of good-natured defiance, flaunting an independent spirit and flouting the petty regulation of food rationing. In short, these and many other war-inspired scripts of the time reflected the attitude of 'islanders' at large, with their approval of any form of anarchy that tiptoes the eccentric line between the assertion of individual rights and downright irresponsibility. Whether this is a good or bad attitude is a matter of opinion but it is likely that the more causeways we build, the more it will be diluted.

What is coincidentally odd is that the only 'real' film that existed at the time about Eriskay, or for that matter any other Hebridean island, had been made by a German. In 1934 Werner Kissling, a former diplomat and one-time member of the elite Prussian Guard, abandoned his homeland and hove to in Acairseid Mhor with a 16mm film camera and a desire to record a world beyond his immediate experience. The twenty-minute film, *A Poem of Remote Lives*, now the property of the Scottish Film Archive, shows a realistic and sympathetic version of Eriskay life as it then was. Unlike many of the patronising travel documentaries of the time, Kissling wanted an authentic picture. The songs and snatches of conversation are in Gaelic and are integral to the film, rather than acting as background atmospherics. The commentary in English explains how the singing encourages a unison of harmony and effort when communal hard work has to be done, and the filming of the *luadh*, or beating of the cloth by the island women, displays it at its most vigorous. It would take a cycle of ten songs for the tweed, which has been soaked in urine, to be pounded into its shrunken finished form. It has to be said that the lyrics, which had a deal to say about the characteristics of the men locally available, were not the usual musical accompaniment to the promotional films released by Caledonian MacBrayne.

Those who retain their imagination and wish to write their own poem can still think of Eriskay as an island. A ferry from the north end of Barra permits a landing by sea and the island is sufficiently compact to be thoroughly explored on foot. The simplest excursion is to take the road from the jetty until it ends at the Big Anchorage. Then return over the moorsides and summit of Ben Scrien to the games room of The Polly. The route is short and the hill is small but, as in Barra, there is a distinct sense of place. What is more, if sufficiently brave, you could check out the provenance of the ponies. Even with the causeway, you will probably have the walk to yourself and if you should do this, you might chance to consider life on a small island. Beset by some of the roughest weather in the world, it offered a variety of ways of meeting a violent end. Being run over wasn't one of them.

A Rum Do

The Cocktail Isles, Rum, Eigg and Muck, stand to the south and slightly west of the mountains of Skye. On the map and from certain viewpoints they resemble various-sized tugs about to tow the larger island and its Cuillin Ridge into sunnier climes – a pipe-dream of all climbers who have received an armful of water every time they reached for a hold in the rain-worn conduits of the Crack of Doom or Waterpipe Gully. The trio is usually defined, more prosaically, as belonging to the Parish of the Small Isles, to allow the fourth and presumably abstemious Canna into their midst.

Although of the quartet Rum takes pride of place, the other three deserve a visit. This is not quite as straightforward as might be imagined. Despite being close to the mainland, they are not easily accessible. The ferry does a round trip from Mallaig but the timetable is rather complicated and liable to change at short notice if an emergency occurs. There is also a lack of harbours capable of handling the ferry, so passengers have to transfer, often precariously, to a 'flit' or tender to complete their journey. There are day trips from Arisaig in the summer and the easiest option is to pick the islands off one by one. If time is limited, the most interesting of the three is Eigg.

From many mountain summits of the western seaboard, Eigg is instantly recognisable. The Sgurr, or coxcomb, stands out as a unique feature. It is a long, narrow platform of rock rearing above the habitation at Galmisdale and surrounded on three sides by steep cliffs that offer no way to the pedestrian. The top, however, is easily reached. At the point where the rock burrows back into the moorland, a gully allows access to the airy ridge. This promenade across the columnar pitchstone terminates at the Sgurr itself. As you would imagine, this provides a fine viewpoint for the greater island hills of Rum and Skye.

The coastline is also worth a look. Among a number of caves is Uamh Fhraing or Massacre Cave. In 1577, the MacLeods of Skye invaded the island to avenge a perceived wrong perpetrated on their clansmen by the local MacDonalds. The inhabitants, man, woman and child, to escape detection hid in the cave. The plan seemed to have worked, for the

MacLeods, finding no one at home, abandoned the raid and set sail. Unfortunately, an over-hasty Mac-Donald put his head above the parapet and was spotted. The MacLeods returned and, having trapped their enemy in the cave, tried to smoke them out by building a brushwood fire in the entrance. The outcome was that every man, woman and child was suffocated. Or so the tale goes.

But none of this compares with the history of the 'Forbidden Island', Rum or variously Rhum. It follows the normal pattern – an expanding community built around the kelp industry to fulfil the demand for potash, demand falling with consequent economic collapse, humans exchanged for sheep, sale to absentee landlord. In this case it was the owner of a manufacturing business in Lancashire who developed it into his private sporting estate. So that no one should interfere with the pleasure of the owner and his guests, visitors were actively discouraged. MacBraynes, who ran a ferry service to the island, had instructions to land only those who had proof of permission to visit. The press got wind of the story and its reputation grew.

John Bullough had acquired his money by building machinery to service the local cotton industry in Accrington. His designs proved superior to those of his competitors and he was soon supplying not only the whole of the county but also exporting abroad to a thriving Empire. On his death, his son George took over the business and the family assets. He realised the value of electricity as a source of power and developed the business in that direction to become one of the richest men in the country. In his spare time, he indulged his two passions – his yacht, Rhouma, which was large enough to serve as a hospital ship in the Boer War, and developing his island kingdom.

His first act was to establish a suitable base. He demolished the rat-infested Kinloch House and, with the help of the London architects Leeming and Leeming, designed and built Kinloch Castle. All turrets and MacTaj Mahal, it is a folly on a grand scale. However, the detail is impressive. Sandstone was the chosen building material and there was plenty to be had near at hand. Bullough, however, did not care for the colour, so imported a nicer shade of pink from the Isle of Arran. In keeping with his Marahajah of the Glen view of the Highlands, he insisted that his 300-strong workforce, much to the delight of the local midge and cleg, undertook the construction work wearing the kilt of the Rum tartan.

On my first visit to the island, I stayed in the hostel accommodation offered at Kinloch Castle. This was, in fact, the servants' quarters and, though sparse, was well appointed with, among other features, secondary glazing. This was merely one of Sir George's inventions. The family firm had been quick to see the commercial advantage that could be gained by the use of electricity and the owner of Kinloch Castle realised that it could also have a variety of domestic uses. The castle was the second place in Scotland to benefit from electric light. The first was Glasgow. Electricity also powered the air-conditioning unit which removed cigar smoke from the billiard room.

Not that Sir George abandoned the tested and tried. The plumbing was both extensive and ingenious. The hot water that it produced fed the *pièce de résistance*, the ultimate bathing machine. This was a bath with a hood at one end, and the intricacy of the pipework allowed any combination of bath, shower, douche and what has come to be known as a jacuzzi to be operated at will. Nor was this ingenuity reserved for the human race. The pipes that provided the central heating extended to the gardens to create a climate that not only encouraged the flourishing of many exotics in the heated glasshouses but also fed the ornamental pools where turtles basked and alligators lurked.

In fact, the garden received as much attention in the planning stage as the building. Tons of topsoil were imported from Ayrshire, along with thousands of trees and plants, comprising over a hundred species. In the daily interface between house and garden, the head gardener was charged with producing a centrepiece for the dining table. This consisted of a small garden complete with soil, rockery, etc, which floral ensemble was resurrected in an entirely different manner each morning. This touch was designed to complement the Steinway concert grand, stained glass windows, cut-glass chandeliers, silk tapestries and, for suitably martial moments, the Orchestrian, a mechanical device that played tunes on a variety of bugles and drums.

The rest of the island also failed to escape Bullough's ingenuity. He created a telephone exchange with ten lines to keep in touch with his 'tacksmen'. He established a laundry at Kilmory at the north end of the island, a round trip of four miles on foot for the unfortunate laundry maids (it is to be assumed that Bullough kept his Rolls Royce for personal excursions), and a family mausoleum in the fashion of a Doric temple at the south and more clement end. One can only conclude that the family took the middle-class interdiction of not hanging out your dirty linen in public all too literally. Perhaps they were wise. Secrecy encourages speculation. There were a variety of rumours, one of the most popular being the use of the Rhouma to ship Gaiety Girls from London for the delight and delectation of Sir George's guests.

But all good things come to an end. And the demise has an irony of its own. The combined effects of the rise in manufacturing industries and the deprivation resulting from the First World War were sufficient to destroy the pool of cheap labour that formed the servant class necessary to man the likes of Kinloch Castle. There was more money and, with the growth of the Trade Union movement, more security and independence in tending the factory loom than every whim of the factory owner. In addition, money made in exporting goods to the Third World dried up, as British prices were undercut. Upkeep became prohibitive and in 1957 the estate was sold to the Nature Conservancy, of which more anon.

While all this was coming and going, the princi-pal attraction of the island, at least to the mountain-eer, remained unchanged. The Rum Cuillin, though not as impressive as the Skye counterpart, was and is worth all the trouble of getting there. The obvi-ous day is the traverse of the main ridge, starting at Kinloch and returning by the Dibidil path. The traverse does not compare in difficulty with that of Skye and although some moderately difficult rock can be found if the watershed is strictly adhered to, all is avoidable. A path from Kinloch leads to the Beallach Bairc Mheall and the ridge itself. This, between Hallival and Askival, is particularly airy and leads to a gabbro scramble which includes the Askival Pinnacle. The ascent of this is a little harder than the rest but is probably easier to climb than avoid. Askival is the highest point of the island and provides a tremendous viewpoint, not only of the neighbouring hills but also those of Barra and South Uist to the west.

I can recall standing in bewilderment on the sum-mit, looking at what appeared to be almost a childish drawing of a mass of mountains peaks spreading in all directions. Although the incubation period was extensive, it was here, I suppose, that I first contracted the virus of Munroitis. Descend the west ridge of Askival to the Bealach an Oir and scramble up the east ridge of Trallval. This has two summits, the west being the higher and separated by another airy ridge. A return is necessary to reach the southern flank that leads to Bealach an Fhuarain. This looks quite difficult, particularly in mist, but is easier than it seems. The same can be said of the ascent of Ainshval. The steep upper reaches can be bypassed to the east and the ridge rejoined by an easy chimney above any difficulties. The rock has now changed from gabbro to Torridonian sandstone and can be less secure when wet, especially in descent. The ridge broadens into a grassy walk to Sgurr nan Gillean, with views down the buttress-strewn Glen Dibidil. The vista was likened, by no less an authority than Sir Hugh Munro, to Glencoe, but more favourably because of the sea views.

The best descent to Dibidil from Sgurr nan Gillean is not the direct east ridge but by the easier south ridge for a thousand feet before you traverse easily to the bothy. From here, you take the six-mile coast path back to Kinloch, a good stretch at the end of a long day. After rain, the walk above the cliff tops offers a dramatic sight, with streams cascading into the sea below. It reaches its high point above Welshman's Rock, so called after the eighteenth-century Welsh masons who cut ledges out of the rock to allow straying sheep to escape. But, rather than complete the circuit in a day, it is a good idea to stay overnight in the bothy and tackle the Dibidil Horseshoe the following morning.

The better way to nail the horseshoe is withershins, first attacking the summit of Beinn nan Stac by the south-east ridge. Provided difficulties are not avoided, the ascent of this and Askival can give a climb not dissimilar to the long easy route from Loch Coruisk up the east side of the peaks of Sgurr Dubh. When two esteemed members of the SMC decided to take the day off from serious climbing and spend the day 'Doing the Dubhs', the club poet penned the appropriate doggerel to the effect that 'viewing the views/And regarding the mountains in mute admiration' was something that should not be forgotten in the process of climbing mountains. This is especially true of Rum. As has already been mentioned, the ridge from Askival to Sgurr nan Gillean is not without vista which can include the sight of an occasional whale.

As well as ridge scrambling, Rum has its share

of proper rock climbing. Although not as extensive as the Skye Cuillin, there are routes on the Harris buttress of Trallval that are between 300 and 400 feet. Early exploration is described by Bill Murray in his book *Undiscovered Scotland*, after a visit to the island with a climbing friend, Michael Ward. As with all of Murray's writing at that time, there is a delicate underlying juxtaposition between the deprivation and discomfort that was a result of his own choice and that which had been inflicted upon him as a prisoner of war. In this case, it becomes part of an extraneous storyline, a technique which Murray habitually uses to prevent the account of his exploits from being little more than a guidebook. When he is joined by his companion, he is surprised to find that, given the trip will last a couple of weeks, Ward is travelling so light. The minimalist explained that the only spare clothing necessary was a sleeping bag, on the grounds that, as you have a waterproof skin, you may as well let your clothes dry out while you are wearing them.

Murray, though envious of this display of hardiness, is sceptical and has taken the precaution of bringing two large rucksacks full of clothes and provisions. In the confusion of the transfer between the ferry and the flit, one of these is left on board and, inevitably, it is the one containing his spare clothing and sleeping bag. Days pass before the ferry returns and Murray has to endure not only nights of damp and cold in the tent at Dibidil but also the knowledge that Ward, with his limited but effective wardrobe, is warm and comfortable. Despite Ward's contribution of his daytime sweater, Murray can only keep warm by controlled bouts of deliberate shivering, a technique that he had developed in various Nazi prison camps.

Their main climbing discovery was Archangel Route on Trallval, so called because the key to success was when Michael, in an act of faith, balanced on the tip of a needle. Re-reading the account, I tried to work out why Murray's descriptions of mountain rock climbs are so successful. There are two schools of thought as to the best approach to the task. On one hand, there is the general: *Climb the series of grooves for 200 hundred feet or so, until a rising traverse allows access to an obvious rib that not only gives magnificent views into the upper corrie but also leads to the top of the crag.* On the other, the specific: *Start two feet left of a large stone that looks when viewed from the east not unlike a Victorian Pillar Box. Climb the slab for fifteen feet with the aid of an intermittent crack until a step to the left allows the use of a good hidden handhold that enables a delicate step onto a large, flat ledge (the Billiard Table), where a variety of belays may be found.*

Both have their drawbacks. In the case of the general, you are left with the uncomfortable feeling that the 'obvious rib' mightn't be that obvious at all and that you could find yourself in uncharted if not irreversible territory. While the specific, unless it is spiced with the gallows humour of such writers as Menlove Edwards, tends to lack literary merit and leaves the climber with the equally uncomfortable feeling that if you don't follow the instructions to the letter you may somehow have cheated and not done the thing at all. Murray seems able to combine the better parts of both. His accounts give a clear picture of the climb as whole, yet manage to convey the detail of the difficulties at particular points on the route. What is more, he makes it exciting. As with *Macbeth*, we may well know the outcome but that does not diminish the anticipation as to how events will unfold.

This little and large approach is also evident when he comes to describe the walking traverse of the Rum hills. At one moment, he is carrying you along the airy ridges with sweeping views in all directions. At another, he is persuading his companion to put his head down a series of rabbit holes to discover the source of a chirping noise within. The key is that, whether on the crux of a new route or crossing the wastes of Rannoch Moor, he makes you feel that you too are there. And this is not simply topographically but also in an emotional and intellectual sense.

The chirping rabbits were, in fact, Manx shearwaters. Graceful in flight and secure in their community rafts at sea, these birds are both clumsy and vulnerable on land. For this reason, they nest in burrows near the top of the mountains where they incubate their single egg and feed the newborn chick. The parental change of guard is only done in the dark of night amidst a cacophony of banshee-like howling. Little wonder the Norse explorers thought it came from the hill of the Trolls. The parents are forced to leave before their offspring can fly, so they fill it to the gunwales before taking off for Brazil. One of the consequences of this parental zeal is that often the chicks are so bloated they can't get out of the burrow and have to remain there until the enforced diet allows them to escape and, after a waddling descent of 1500 feet down the cliffs, reach the sea where, if they are lucky, they will find further sustenance.

Rum, given the comparative absence of undue interference, is, not surprisingly, a lucky haven for wildlife of all kinds. One visitor reported seeing in the space of a few minutes after landing on the island a goldcrest, a golden eagle and a corncrake, birds that many people never see in a lifetime. Once the Nature Conservancy Council had ownership of the island and decided to use it as a living laboratory, it appeared that matters for the locals could only get better. Any potential interference could be controlled and sensitive areas carefully monitored. As a result, a variety of studies unearthed a range of species that had lived for the most part unnoticed.

The major study carried out, or at least the most obvious, concerns the island's herd of deer. To achieve this, large chunks of Rum are closed to the general public and access is restricted. Much has been done to determine the optimum cull and this, with other observation of animals, tagged for life, has produced evidence that is of supposed benefit to the venison industry. One of the surprising facts to emerge is that the animals are occasionally carnivorous, eating fledgling seabirds. As, I presume, all this is paid for out of the public purse, it might be worth considering the worth of the enterprise. The scientist will argue that pushing back the boundaries of knowledge is sufficient reason in its own right. But is it a properly conducted scientific experiment? There seems to be an air of artificiality in pretending that man doesn't exist and the sight of the frontier-busters stalking baby deer with overgrown butterfly nets can appear a little bizarre. Perhaps a couple of packs of wolves could be introduced. After all, it was man who killed them off. You could argue there should be one or the other.

There has been one move in this direction and that is the re-introduction of the sea eagle, the last of which had been shot by Bullough's gamekeeper. The birds were brought in as fledglings from Norway and are now well established, much to the delight of many. But even this wheel might be going full circle. Sea eagles, unlike deer (or even wolves), cannot be contained. Breeding pairs have left the island and set up house in less conserved areas. The lambing season coincides with the eagles' young being hatched and when there are hungry mouths to be fed, the new-born lamb can be a tempting sight. It is, therefore, not altogether surprising that the birds on the mainland have died after eating carcasses that could well have been poisoned.

Perhaps nothing has really changed after all. Who or whatever is in charge of Bullyboys Hall seems in a position to play God, or at least lay down the ground rules to suit its own purposes. Most lovers of the countryside are more than pleased to see the monarchs of the glen and sky given freedom to roam, but what will be their reaction if this seriously curtails their own opportunity? No one especially wants to visit Gruinard Island but what if the Skye Cuillin or the great glens of Affric, Cannich and Strathfarrar suddenly became Sites of Special Scientific Interest? And, anyway, who's standing a corner for the Rum rats, which at one time were so populous that they successfully drove the majority of the inhabitants off the island for good?

Mingulay

Mingulay

When I began to consider this chapter, I recalled two events much separated by time and space. The first was a rendering of the Mingulay Boat Song at a ceilidh held in Barra's Castlebay Hotel, where the rise and fall of a slightly sibilant voice and an insistent underlying rhythm had combined to create the sound and mood of the sea. The second was a childhood book of nursery rhymes which, as you turned the page, triggered a musical box to play the appropriate tune. Perhaps, I thought, the easiest way to describe the island, or at least my impression of it, was to persuade the publishers to insert a similar device which sprang into action at the suitable moment.

Sad to say, this flight of imaginative legerdemain had no substance. The tune came not from the misty isles but was a Lochaber hunting song turned by Hugh Robertson into a sea shanty for the Glasgow Orpheus Choir. He only chose the trisyllabic 'Mingulay' because he thought it might be chorally useful. As for the nursery rhymes, they too fell apart as an inquisitive mind and clumsy fingers investigated the workings of that particular box of tricks. So are illusions shattered. Though, I suppose, 'The Grand Old Duke of York' might have kickstarted my interest in peak bagging.

Even Mingulay is not what it was. At its peak, it held 150 inhabitants, a school and a church. In common with other islanders, they survived by catching fish. But their speciality was collecting the eggs and young of the various seabirds that lived on the cliffs and sea stacks that form the western side of the island. As with the good Doctor's gradation of red wine, so were the jobs divided. The boys caught puffins by laying snares outside their burrows or 'fished' from the cliff-tops with nooses attached to long poles. The men descended the precipices on ropes made from horsehair, hanging on with one hand, collecting their catch with other. But to those who aspired to the brandy fell the most dangerous task of all. The technique was to sail a boat close to the cliffs of a sea stack and, using the swell, leap for a small and no doubt slippery ledge. The foremost hero, called the *Gingich*, carried a rope to assist the party in making a safe landing, then led the way up the rock. The rest followed with suitable receptacles. The tricky bit was the return. Here the leader had to jump into the bobbing boat as it was buffeted by the violent seas, before securing it alongside to allow a steadier retreat for the others.

In fact, you have to be a bit of a *gingich* yourself, if you want to visit the island. Mingulay's greatest problem was that it didn't have a natural harbour and launching and beaching the fishing boats required the crews to wade chest-high into the sea. Pleas for a slipway were ignored. My own experience of landing, on a day trip from Barra, was of the boat pulling into a rocky inlet where visitors had to scramble with care onto nearish-by ledges.

Because the boatman will be understandably cautious, your time on the island may be short and it is best to plan in advance. The remains of the village are interesting and worthy of a lengthy study in their own right. But it would be a pity to miss the remainder of the island, particularly the cliffs and stacks of the west coast. The best view is from Dun Mingulay, a steep-sided peninsula rising 300 feet above the sea and joined to the mainland by a narrow isthmus. Somewhere below you is a cave where James Grant, a Catholic priest, hid after the battle of Culloden and in another, so rumour has it, is a treasure of French gold intended to fund the army of Charles Edward Stuart. If time permits, visits to Hecla, Carnan, Tom a' Mhaide and Macphee's Hill make a fine round. You could split this itinerary over two separate visits, but, as many have found, Mingulay is not an easy place to get onto.

Or get off. When you reach Macphee's Hill, it is as well to check that your transport home is still available. Otherwise you might suffer the same fate as the poor lad after whom the hill is named. Mac-Neil of Barra, realising that he had not received his rent from the tenants on Mingulay for some time, sent in the bailiffs to investigate. As they approached the island, they could see no sign of life. To be on the safe side, they despatched Macphee, the young-est member of the crew, to wade ashore and report back. In due course, he returned to say that he had been to the village and found nothing but corpses. Fearing the plague, his colleagues immediately set sail and left Macphee to his fate. There he remained for a year and a day, sleeping in a remote rocky cleft and surviving on shellfish. He spent his days perched on his soon-to-be-eponymous hill, trying to attract the attention of passing boats. Eventually MacNeil relented and allowed the boy's father to investigate and Macphee was saved. That's how the tale goes, but I've heard as many versions as tellers.

The island was repopulated and the Macphees were given land free of rent for their trouble and for a time all went well. But times change. Ironically, the Clearances caused overcrowding as escapees fled to this inaccessible island. A bout of typhus sapped the islanders' morale. Eyes were cast abroad. First to the fertile soil of nearby Vatersay. Then, as education and communications improved, to the paid labour of mainland Scotland. By 1912, the island was left to the sheep. It must have seemed as if the other inhabited islands would, like falling dominoes, suffer Mingulay's fate. However, help came from an unexpected source. Thatcherism, that did so much social and economic damage to industrial Britain, meant there was considerably less work available in the north of the kingdom. This encouraged the islanders, faced with the choice between Billericay and Berneray, to decide to return home. As it was put to me: *If you're going to be unemployed, you may as well be unemployed with a view.*

On the Rock

A fter a couple of teenage summer holidays, Phil and I realised that we had climbed all the worthwhile hills in the Lake District, though I suppose our definition of 'worthwhile' corresponded exactly to the hills we had actually climbed. A greater challenge was sought. This duly arrived in the form of a brochure from Tyrolean Travel Ltd, which, with dramatic photographs, offered an 'unforgettable holiday in the Austrian Alps'.

The trip was a success but, in its course, suggested that there were a couple of areas that had to be dealt with if we were to make any further progress in the mountaineering business, i.e. we had to work out how to deal with the white stuff and, equally significantly, accept that the ascent of certain hills required something a little more technical than a head-down, knees-up approach. We tackled the first problem *in situ* with a visit to the local *Eispickelgeschäft*, where we purchased ice-axe and crampons at under £2 a head, followed by appropriate practice on some not too ferocious snow slopes. There was one unnerving moment on a summit snowfield when some steps that we were following suddenly stopped in thin air, as it were. But generally we seemed to cope.

The second was more problematic. By the end of the fortnight there were still some rocky summits that lay untouched. Even in our most self-deluding moments we could not fool ourselves that we had climbed every 'worthwhile' hill in the Stubai. There had been times when we had turned back for no other reason than that it looked too difficult and/or dangerous to continue. Although we had ethical doubts as to the exact position of petrogymnastics in the canon of Real Mountaineering, it was clear that the time had come to take up rock climbing. The question was not so much how, as where.

We knew no one who climbed and the local library was limited in its support. It extolled the virtues of bracing mountain air but warned against the folly of straying too close to the edge. Local bookshops were too busy offloading copies of *Lady Chatterley's Lover* to take an interest in less horizontal matters. Then a friend, a keen cyclist, recalled that the emporium where he purchased his water bottles and bicycle clips had a small niche where there was 'rope and stuff'. Thither we resorted and bought what appeared the complete stock, to wit: 120 feet of nylon rope, two full-weight slings complete with karabiners and, *mirabile dictu*, a Lake District climbing guide entitled *Pillar Rock*.

The miracle was that it was there at all. For, as we were to discover, our interest in the sport coincided with a dearth of climbing guidebooks. Why this was so was not clear at the time. It was only later we discovered that in the fifties there had been an explosion within the sport. Rock climbing, previously the property of the Old Universities and a handful of local enthusiasts, had been taken over by an invasion from the industrial towns and cities of Lancashire and Yorkshire. Young men armed with motorbikes and fresh techniques acquired on the local gritstone tackled routes on the big cliffs that previously had been considered untenable and rendered existing guidebooks (with or without bikes) woefully out of date. Clogwyn du'r Arddu is a prime example. The last guide had been written in 1942 and contained little more than a dozen climbs that tackled the main buttresses. When the new guide was produced twenty years later (one reviewer thought it, as a read, more exciting than the latest Bond novel) there were a further fifty climbs, all at a very high standard. The same was true of the Lake District. Langdale, the most accessible area for the masses, had a climbing guide published in 1950 and had to wait until 1967 for an update.

It seemed that guidebook production had ground to a halt. There would have been little point in reprinting the out-of-date version and the task of updating must have seemed daunting with its Forth Bridge implications. The senior climbing clubs traditionally had taken the responsibility of producing the old guides and there were probably few of the establishment who were up to the job and, moreover, such few were probably more interested in being part of the ebullition than checking the pitch lengths of such classics as *OVERGROWNANDUSUALLYWET GULLY – 120 feet of rock interspersed amongst several furlongs of potentially lethal grass and scree. Moderately Difficult. Rubbers not recommended. Nevertheless has a certain charm.*

There may have been other reasons – shortage of paper, etc – but the outcome as far as I could see was that guidebooks appeared for sale with the same regularity as hens' teeth. An obsessive consequence of this deprivation was that for a long time I could not resist obtaining any guidebook I came across. There are not many who can boast among their collection of climbing literature a neatly clipped and stapled guide to Twisleton Scar or a handwritten version of the climbs at Rainster and Harborough Rocks, faithfully transcribed from the single reference copy at Nottingham Central Library.

Whatever the reason, the outcome was clear. If we wanted to go rock climbing and engage the reasonable protection that a guidebook afforded, the alpha and omega of our immediate ambition had to be Pillar Rock. We had undertaken a preliminary and generally unsatisfactory skirmish top-roping a local sandstone outcrop but it was soon apparent that this was not the real thing. Our pleasure in discovering handholds, slabs and potential belay points, as described in our teach-yourself manual, was somewhat tempered by the unflattering attention of small boys and a tendency for the rock to come away in substantial handfuls. There was no alternative but come one Easter to set off for Wasdale Head.

In our fellwalking days we had prided ourselves on travelling light. To guard against the cold, we merely moved faster and when it rained we donned the placable pac-a-mac. Of course, this item stopped at the neck but the introduction of the jiffy-hood to the nation's high streets resolved the interim problem. It goes without saying that we did not possess a rucksack between us. So the climbing gear and change of clothes had to be carefully stored in a hold-all apiece. After some discussion, despite the Abrahams' pictures of fearsome-looking men wielding them on vertiginous rock, we dispensed with the *eispickels*. So accoutred, we left the bus at Seatoller in the rain and set off across Sty Head to that Mecca of British Mountaineering, the Wastwater Hotel.

We were in pole position, relaxing over our post-prandial pint, when we realised that another decision had to be made. The summit of Pillar Rock was our objective but the question was by which route. We had felt it prudent to start at a grade termed 'Difficult' so, if it was to be a climb of any length, the choice was limited. It had to be either the North Climb or the New West Climb. The former was discarded after a discussion with a couple of our fellow guests who had that day experienced an epic on the Nose, followed by an undignified collapse into Savage Gully. By comparison, the New West seemed relatively straightforward. I had also read somewhere that it had been named the 'New' West as a delicate

Pillar Rock

compliment to John Atkinson who reputedly made the first ascent of the rock in 1826 by what is now known as the Old West Route. That seemed to add a sense of propriety to the venture.

We were left with a final problem of semantics. How difficult was 'Difficult'? Or, more to the point, was 'Difficult' too difficult? This concern was compounded by the description of the penultimate pitch: *40 feet. A <u>difficult</u> slab is climbed to a rock stance at its right-hand upper corner.* If we arrived at this point and found 'difficult' was in fact too difficult, we would be in an interesting position, i.e. 200 feet off the ground and seventy feet from the top. We decided to shorten the odds against disaster by making a final decision when we reached pitch 6: *A <u>fairly</u> difficult groove.* If this proved to be at the limit of our powers, we would beat an ignominious retreat and take up golf. If not, ever upwards.

The next day was overcast and the traverse along the High Level was accompanied by the fine mist that has appeared on most of my visits to Pillar. A pause at Robinson's Cairn gave us our first look at the problem. A great mass of rock – but, from that side, not as threatening as the rocky spires of the Kalkkogel. We circumnavigated its bulk. The view of the west face was rather different. This seemed a serious slab of rock but the first fifty feet looked and were perfectly reasonable and we soon reached the foot of the defining groove without alarm. I was half-way up this when I was surprised to be overtaken by someone climbing the rib a few feet to my left and obviously heading for the same point of anchorage. I had no idea where they had come from and this general frolicking around seemed to be rather cavalier in what we were regarding as a serious undertaking. Later investigation showed that the Rib and Slab Climb joins the New West at this point.

There was a macramé moment when both parties clustered on the same stance but fortunately the interlopers knew what they were doing and quickly departed. Before they did, I thought it politic to ask about the 'difficult' slab. *No problem – there are a couple of good runners*, was the apparent reassurance. Runners? The only runners we knew about were the likes of Roger Bannister or a less than inspiring vegetable so it didn't really help too much. Once they had climbed past me, I was further confused to notice that they were not wearing proper mountain boots but what appeared to be gym shoes.

Yet, half reassured by the fact that the 'fairly difficult groove' had proved reasonably amenable, we pushed on to the obvious security of a nearby chimney. The half, however, shrank when Phil announced that he had found, secured to the rock, what appeared to be a first aid kit consisting of a bottle of blood plasma. It seemed an odd venue. Was this where most of the cragfast were likely to expire? An offer of appeasement to the local vampires? In retrospect, it probably spurred us on and we found we had done the 'difficult slab' before we realised we had reached it. I suppose the absence of athletes breasting the tape must have caused the confusion. All that remained was a little chimney that popped us out onto the very tip of High Man—two rabbits out of their burrow.

There are certain epiphany-like moments which you will not only never forget but which also can add a dimension to your existence. The arrival at the top of Pillar Rock was such a one for me. Finding the names under a box under the cairn, walking the coastline of this particular island, peering over edges, finding the start, or rather finish, of the Slab and Notch Climb for the 'easy' descent, suggested a world that might hold my attention for a very long time. We traversed into Jordan Gap and tentatively pawed at some cracks described in our bible as Severe (hard) but they were a technique too far at this stage of our development.

Not to worry. We had done the New West and for a first climb, though more through luck than judgement, we couldn't have chosen better. It is hard to define a classic route but this particular excursion would be difficult to beat as an example. It has the prerequisites of sound rock and secure belays. It offers pitches of varying types linked by a couple of traverses and it finishes at the highest point of the cliff. Above all, it offers no form of escape. The rock on either side of it is steeper and blessed with fewer holds. It is a route in the proper sense of the word—a doorway to a secret garden. The question of technical difficulty must be relative. Generally such a climb should be sufficiently difficult to engage your attention but not so hard as to threaten your enjoyment. For some, this is a wallow in the adjectival trough; for others, a taste of the E numbers is required before the adrenalin starts to flow.

We returned in good spirits. I prefer the remoter crags with a longish journey home. The weather patterns in this country often mean that if the day has been dull and wet, the front will pass through and leave a window of sunlight in the early evening. Even if the day has not gone exactly as planned, such an occurrence can make the effort worthwhile. Climbing walls may offer greater intellectual and physical challenges but somehow miss the moment. Anyway, at this point in the game, we were not short of challenges. For a start, there was the Abrahams' photograph of the climber poised on the crux of Eagle's Nest Direct that, in the hotel's dining-room, so dominated the wall and now my imagination.

I, of course, was not the first person to be intrigued by Pillar Rock. This particular geophysical feature has long attracted the attention and excited the thoughts of locals and offcomers alike. Hutchinson's *History of Cumberland* (1794) mentions the 'scowling rocks and precipices'. Green in his guide of 1819 lays it on with a trowel:

Turning from the lake to the mountains, and the dale, which beyond the enclosures becomes narrow, the Pillar assumes even greater importance. From the foot and sides of the lake, its rude sides, softened by distance and air, appeared only indications of what, on a nearer approach, became more terribly palpable. Frightful would be the vision to the timid

*or those unaccustomed to sights like these, and awful
to all men if instantaneously transported from even
meadows to such rugged uplands, particularly as
seen immediately above the path, where in savage
startings, from the mountain's side, the rocks are like
huge towers falling from immense fortifications.*

But, long before this, the Rock had been given the
ultimate tick of approval, the Wordsworthian kite-
mark of Tourist Authenticity. In 'The Brothers', published in 1800, he pens the following description:

*You see yon precipice; it wears the shape
Of a vast building made of many crags;
And in the midst is one particular rock
That rises like a column from the vale,
Whence by our shepherds is called the Pillar.*

What added to the allure, even in modern times,
was the Rock's relative inaccessibility. Most visitors
reached the Lakes from the south or east but Pillar
lies at the head of Ennerdale, which is in the north-
west of the district. What is more, the dale had no
public road, which necessitated a long walk in and a
steep pull to the foot of the cliffs. If you stayed at the

popular climbing centres, you had to climb out of one valley and traverse into another and a good proportion of the day was spent in getting to and from your objective. To some, this is part of the charm, to others, apparently not. Of the times I have visited the Rock, we have, more often than not, been the only party there. Perhaps even the shepherds shun it. After all, their eponymous crag is less than fifty yards from the road and flanked by a public bar on either side.

Eventually the summit was conquered. As mentioned, the first ascent is credited to John Atkinson in 1826. But one is tempted to suspect that the absolute authenticity of this might have been to a certain extent media-manufactured, as the *Cumberland Advertiser* and the *Carlisle Patriot* both contained an identical paragraph describing the event. The existence of a wall on the east side of Low Man, which was designed to stop sheep straying and becoming cragfast, shows earlier human activity. Although there is no evidence that any of these shepherds tried to continue by what became known as the Old Wall Route, it would be very unlike human nature if no one had thought of giving it a go. But no one contradicted Atkinson's claim, as they most surely would have done if there had been a competition between the locals.

There was also the feeling amongst the powers that be that shepherds didn't really count and the first sporting ascent of the true amateur was made by Lieutenant Wilson RN in 1847 and duly recorded as such. I am not quite sure why the climbing establishment frowned on shepherds. Perhaps it felt that they couldn't be trusted. They might employ unethical methods, such as combined tactics with pyramids of sheep or other by hook-or-by-crook contrivances. By 1875, there had been some 119 separate ascents and, with the arrival of W P Haskett Smith, fresh from his success on Napes Needle, the assault on the Rock from various angles and directions began in earnest.

The difficulties these early pioneers experienced are easily forgotten. Even eventually sound passages were beset by loose rock. Haskett Smith and his brother were trying to work out a route on the north face which in due course was to become the North Climb. Beaten by a particularly awkward section, they decided to retreat. Haskett Smith slid down a large block resting against the main face. Suddenly the block began to heel over on top of him. He explains the outcome in an article in the 1892 *Alpine Journal*:

Letting go with my right hand, I rolled over on my left side, wrenched my waistcoat free of the stone, and hung over the precipice by my left hand only. If the stone did not fall quickly I was lost. It seemed to hesitate but then came slowly over. My right hand seizing the tottering mass and weighing heavily upon it eased for a moment the strain upon my left; then as the great stone dipped for its first plunge my right foot swinging up on to it and kicking viciously downwards gave sufficient upward impetus to enable my right hand once more to clutch the hold above. It was a near thing; but a moment later I swung into the cleft just vacated by the stone. I felt, rather than heard, my late enemy thundering down into the valley, and meanwhile someone near me grunting and gasping out, αυτις επειτα πεδονδε κυλινδετο λαας αναιδης.[1] The grunter was myself.

1. *'Instantly back again bounded the merciless rock to the bottom'* is the outcome of the eternal failure of Sisyphus to complete the task of pushing a boulder to the top of a hill before his strength failed.

It would be interesting to compare a modern-day imprecation under similar circumstances. Perhaps an appropriate hexameter from Bob Dylan's 'Like a Rolling Stone'.

By the time the centenary of the first ascent was celebrated, there were no less than thirty-five distinct and different ways to the top. That Easter Sunday in 1926 would have been an extraordinary sight to earlier generations. Scores of people had found their way to the summit to celebrate Atkinson's feat. In addition, those who were still too 'timid or unaccustomed to sights like these' sat on the fellside looking across Jordan, if not at a band of angels, at least at the promised land. A contemporary description likened them to seabirds perched on a sea cliff. And in a sense they were, looking out from the mainland to the insular and often mist-girt stack of Pillar.

Don't!!
Waste Words
Jump to Conclusions

Dalton

At the end of the nineteenth century, a man gave up his job in London and went to live in a tent. Not out of circumstance but out of choice. The man was a lover of mountains and therefore it is not surprising that he was a member of the Fell & Rock Climbing Club. What is surprising is that in the Club's membership list he gave his address as 'The Camp', Billericay, Essex – the least interesting part of Britain for the mountaineer. This, however, was merely the first step and for the remainder of his life, eschewing conventional habitation, he lived either in a cave in the Lake District or, for winter quarters, in Epping Forest.

Donne may well be right in his opinion as to the contiguous nature of man, in that there has to be a point, material, emotional or spiritual, to which he is attached. But there are some who deliberately dissociate themselves from a world they see pulling in the wrong direction. They are people who realise, like the guest at one of Tom Eliot's cocktail parties, that walking the opposite way to the crowd is not perforce making a mistake. Although not necessarily insular, they are insulated and, if you hold the glass to the light at the right angle, they might well be described as islands. Such a man was Millican Dalton.

The cave he lived in was amongst the old lead workings in Castle Crag, The Jaws of Borrowdale, Nr Keswick – and that, if such a thing was needed, was the address of his summer residence. Not that his life depended on such sophistications of communication and when rarely it did, he placed his addressed letter in the post-box without the unnecessary encumbrance of an envelope. His general philosophy was expressed by the slightly ambiguous legend expertly carved at the cave entrance: *Dont!! Waste Words, Jump to Conclusions.*

His lifestyle was self-sufficient. He made his own clothes and a little money by manufacturing lightweight camping equipment for others. All who knew him commented on the ingenuity of his domestic arrangements. He styled himself the Professor of Adventure and had great enthusiasm for his subject. He would lead like-minded groups into various escapades, climbing waterfalls in spate, exploring caves and shooting rapids on his home-made raft.

To those who cared to listen, he expounded his views on Life, the Universe and the Virtues of the Alfresco. An article written for an early *Fell & Rock Journal* extolled:

One of my favourite camps is a steep fellside in Borrowdale commanding a perfect view of a perfect lake... I have watched many gorgeous sunsets from this spot, as we cooked over our wood fire and dined in the open. On one such occasion we reclined in our red blankets, gazing over the ever-changing tints of the sky, yellow, orange, crimson, pink and grey, merging into the blue, purple and violet of the hills — all these colours duplicated in the lake beneath.

He goes on to describe the exploits of 'The Savage Club', both in the Lakes and elsewhere, and is particularly insistent on the medicinal benefits of the open-air life which 'has been found by experience to be a cure, not a cause, of rheumatism, as it is likewise for consumption and neurasthenia'. As he lived to the age of eighty and died still planning expeditions for the coming year, he would have argued that he was the proof of his (as many must have believed) pudding-head theories.

He took parties of all ages and (to the consternation of some) both sexes camping and climbing. His preferred routes seem to have been on the south-facing crag of Great Gable, the Needle being a particular favourite. There was some sense in this. If you are going to spend a considerable time on stances cajoling beginners up the ridges of Eagle, Abbey and Arrow, you might as well make as much of the sunshine as is available.

However, the tour *de force* was his introduction into the mysteries of Doves Nest Crag. This cliff on the slopes of Glaramara was as different from the orthodox climbing crag as Dalton was from the orthodox climber. At one stage in its geological history, a huge rock face had split from the parent mountain. But instead of crashing down into the valley and shattering into a hundred pieces, it tottered and, as though weary of adolescent rebellion, leant back against its progenitor. The result was that in the angle between parent and child lay a series of fissures, cracks and chambers that caused a sort of superterranean pothole. The names of the routes – The Rat Hole, Attic Cave, The Belfrey – give an indication of the norm but a surprising twist is given as the climber is, from time to time, forced onto the exposure of an open face before retreating once more into the security of its innards. Dalton delighted in showing his guests round, illuminating hidden recesses by letting drop blazing pieces of newspaper and warning of the acoustic nature of the labyrinth should they accidentally strike their head on an invisible roof.

Not that this was his only showpiece. From his own front door, he would lead visitors up a scrambly ridge to the summit of Castle Crag. Before them, the host had laid out not only a view of the highest fells, Skiddaw, Helvellyn, Scafell, with their connecting corridors of Greenup and Langstrath to complement the sweep of dale and Derwentwater, but also, as one guest put it, his own backgarden of 'Johnny Wood and High Doat, and lovely Charity Coppice with its never failing stream and secret waterfall which has its source in Rigg Head and Scawdel'.

This knowledge of Millican Dalton comes not from personal experience – he died a year or two before my first visit to the area – but, in the first instance, from the writings of Harry Griffin. Griffin's books not only were an inspiration to leave the beaten track (you don't often find people queuing to climb on Boat Howe Crag) but they also taught me an important literary lesson. If you are going to write

81

about *The Real Wherever*, you must do more than concentrate on descriptions of landscape. You should have a troupe of people, memories and events that you can bring on stage at the theatrically significant moment. The adventurous professor has proved a useful member of the cast.

But though I never knew Dalton, he rang a bell, a past echo, half-remembered. It was only when I came to write this piece that I realised that I had connected him with my childhood reading of Arthur Ransome, so many of whose books were set in the Lake District. I would like to think that Ransome may well have known or heard of Dalton – they were of an age – and used him as the basis for certain adult males that appear in his books. These were the eccentric avuncular types that allow the children credible participation in a grown-up world: the well-travelled uncle who has firsthand experience of mining for gold or the charcoal burners who live in a wigwam and keep a snake in a cigar box for luck. There are also, intriguingly, overlapping points of detail that appear in both histories – the heavily laden bicycle, a boat with a single red sail, Peter Duck's cave.

On his death, Dalton received, not the usual

obituary in the *Fell & Rock Journal* but, more fittingly, a commemorative article entitled 'Memories of my First Leader', written by Mabel Barker, the first woman to climb Central Buttress on Scafell. Amongst these memories, she recalled a time when she invited her mentor to stay at Friar Row. Her consequent dilemma seems to catch the nature of the man:

It was a problem whether it would do him the greater honour and pleasure to put him in the best bedroom or the garage – I forget which it was; probably a tent in the garden!

Winter Holiday

The house at Brevig had two windows in its roof. The windows looked east over Brevig Bay. Under each window was a deep sill on which the children, in perhaps an act of sacrificial barter, had laid out their meagre allowance of most valued toys, each precisely placed in a private island. Looking through either window revealed the same view – a graceful curve covered with a grey carpet that stirred slightly when the prevailing wind sneaked around the protecting hillside. As daylight diluted the gloom, the sky grew less charcoal and soon the sea and sky reached a monotonous harmony that revealed nothing.

The ratchet of the earth clicked another notch, straining for the sun and the consequent sea-change. First, a brownish-red sliced across the horizon. Then, as if a theatrical conjuror had thrown a switch, a haemorrhage of crimson. The inner isles, previously invisible, were thrown in sharp relief, a squadron of night-black icebergs tethered on a vermilion sea.

Another notch and they were gone, flushed away by an act of different brilliance which swept across the bay, flicking the tips of waves that rubbed against the skerries. Houses around the bay hunched, waiting for the time to pass to Christmas.

The decision to spend the festive season on Barra had not been taken heavily. The mid-seventies window of sunshine that had tempted the British to holiday at home had even extended its parasol to the northern extremities of the British Isles. So the memories of silver sands and Hebridean sunsets held sway. What better way to spend the tide of Christmas than on the backwash of a shared enthusiasm? The self-catering accommodation was re-booked at a fraction of the summer rate and, as usual, the detail was forgotten.

The first little nudge that matters might be a little more complex was the arrival of Caledonian MacBrayne's winter timetable. The sailings no longer assumed boatloads of holidaymakers arriving on the Glasgow train, but had moved into a more workaday mode. This meant a more complex rail journey from Macclesfield and, if you were to catch the morning ferry, an overnight stay in Oban. However, as these were the pre-Thatcherite days of public transport, you could still assume that what was published by way of a timetable tended to happen on the ground and there seemed no real reason for concern.

To say that the journey went without a hitch would be less than accurate. The weight of carrying Christmas to the Outer Hebrides caused a spectacular explosion of a bottle of sauce and the rending of an ageing rucksack strap in the ten-and-a-half seconds allowed for the change at Preston. The latter was not as inconvenient as might be assumed. When standing on the ground, the rucksack reached chest level. If you are manoeuvring such a piece of baggage through doors, along passages and around light-fittings, you tend to have to manhandle rather than shoulder your responsibilities. The outcome of the former is best glossed over.

The interchange at Glasgow was also interesting. The paterfamilias, feeling that he had borne the burden of the enterprise, repaired to the Red Roy MacGregor bar and, as Scottish law forbade the appearance of children, the rest of the troupe made do with the cafeteria. It is an immutable law of liquid consumption that it takes longer to drink beer than Coke. The result is an corresponding imbalance of absorption. The Coke finished, minds become absorbed in other matters and the matter in hand, as far as the larger section of the party was concerned, was whether we would miss the connection. I believe in punctuality but see little point in arriving early, particularly if there are more pressing concerns. So when I reappeared, my daughter was giving her very best Orphan Annie impression, much to the concern of the inhabitants of Queen Street Station. The said residents tend not from the most salubrious section of Glasgow's society and their choice of wine is dictated rather by circumstance than appellation, but even they found it impossible to comprehend the depths of depraved irresponsibility to which I must have sunk to create such concern in a child. I left the concourse with, no doubt, not just a metaphorical flea in my ear.

And it was in such a way that, two days before Christmas, we arrived in Oban. If you were to ask me what Oban was like at that time of year, my reply would be, *shut*. One of the few hotels that had opened a sufficient chink to allow a skeleton staff to slip through was a relic of the glory days of travel. Panelled oak doors protected the most meagre of chambres and draperies abounded. But there the service ended. Breakfast consisted of tired croissants and do-it-yourself teabags and as we slipped out of a side door into the early morning darkness the first little niggle of doubt, that there might be a bit more to this than I had anticipated, began to tap on my shoulder.

What would happen if Barra was as shut as Oban? The reason for the oversized rucksack was the necessity for, or at least the insistence that, anything traditionally associated with Christmas, i.e. crackers, cake, pudding, presents (I drew the line at tree) was within, so the food we had with us was more celebratory than functional. We had assumed to buy the staff of life bit on arrival. If the shop were to be shut, we could either surfeit on mince pies or be forced into a four-mile round trip to buy fund-consuming hotel meals. To compound matters, Christmas and the weekend coincided in such a way that, as no ferry was due, the shop might remain shut for the best part of a week.

It was, therefore, with more than usual interest that we peered into the gloom as the boat swung into the bay. At this time of the year, the ferry was re-routed from its normal non-stop journey to take in a shoal of small islands and we were about to finish as we had started – in the dark. You tend to forget how far north the northern bits of Britain really are. The Orkneys, for example, are nearer the Arctic Circle than they are to London and the shortest day tends to be shorter than most. The shop, given a local need to safeguard against possible drought, was of course open.

A winter visit to Barra differed from summer in two particular ways. The first I had to a greater or lesser extent anticipated. The rough pasture was now the winter quarters of fieldfares and redwing and Loch Tangasdale was for the same reason covered with a raft of whooper swans. The perpetually low winter sun struck different angles from those of summer and previously blurred edges and planes of land and seascape were now thrown into a sharper and more menacing relief. As the weather was set fair, I considered the easiest way to survey the scene was to walk round the island by its fourteen miles of road. I left Castlebay in a clockwise direction and walked over the col that separated the village from the Atlantic coast.

Near the top of the hill lies a collie. It appears to spend all its waking life lying in the gateway of its owner's house, assessing the passers-by. If such is a pedestrian, it will bark more out of a sense of duty than threat, at the approach of a bicycle it will get to its feet and make a half-hearted attempt to alarm the rider, but the appearance of a motor car offers the real challenge. At first, it seems uninterested but, when the rear wheels are parallel with the gateway, it catapults itself at the nearside tyre and attempts to drag it off its rim. As the road is steep and narrow at this point, cars, particularly if driven by tourists, travel slowly and the collie is able to satisfy the demands of some basic instinct for several yards before the startled driver can pull clear. It reminded me of an old man in my childhood who similarly lurked and, as if from nowhere, leapt in front of unsuspecting motorists brandishing a stick in wild gesticulation at what he considered the nadir of civilisation. Like the collie, he did not risk such demonstrations when the oncoming traffic had gravity in its favour.

The only person I met on my circumnambulation was a man carrying a bottle of whisky. He hailed me as if it were an agreed rendezvous and, grabbing me by the arm with one hand, he unscrewed the top of the bottle with the fingertips of the other. After taking a generous swig himself, he invited me to join him. As it was still early in the morning and whisky is not particularly to my taste, especially when taken in gulps out of a bottle, I declined. At this, he appeared rather upset and the note of disappointment suggested that this was not the first drink of the day. So I thought it best to appease this ancient mariner and by concealing the neck of the bottle with my hand went through the charade of having a drink. Thus, by simultaneously returning the bottle and bidding my farewells, I was able to escape without further molestation.

Along with vengeful collies, this is another of the hazards of Barra. The men are generous with their drink and become offended if rejected. I have no problem with this if the offer consists of beer or even, at a pinch, lager but, as I have indicated, whisky as a regular dosage is not my cup of tea. And as I turned eastward and towards the bar at North Bay, the recent meeting resurrected a current problem that niggled at the back of my mind. This also concerned the said amber liquid. At the end of my last stay, in a maze of goodbyes and goodlucks, I had found myself surrounded by a sea of the stuff as I seemed to have been included in everybody's round. I excused my temperance on the grounds that the ferry left at crack of dawn and that I would finish them off on my next visit. This off-the-cuff attempt at humour caused much deliberation and discussion. At last, a more dirigible than balloon brandy glass was produced, the whisky decanted and a piece of clingfilm stretched across the rim. Then, like some sacred relic, it was placed in the centre of the top shelf behind the bar, *for next time, mind!*

Next time had arrived and as I entered I saw that the balloon was still there and it seemed to contain even more than I had remembered. Fortunately, the donors were out at work, making what they could of the remaining light. The barmaid looked at me, then looked at the whisky, then looked again – I supposed accusingly – in my direction. I nodded as a token of admission. *Will you be having it now?* The tone implied that it was not the most convenient of ornaments. I declined but, assuring her that I would probably deal with it later, finished my pint and left.

I had hardly gone a hundred yards when I met yet again my counter-orbiter. The whisky bottle was still clutched in his hand but was now quite empty. His earlier *bonhomie* had gone and he stood in the middle of the road in the manner of a Hollywood gunslinger, though still with an air of Coleridge about him. The nub of the story, as far as I could gather, was that he had no whisky left. The reason that he had no whisky left was because he had met an Englishman who had drunk it all, or at least the vast part of it. What is more, he could get no more whisky because he had no more money and he couldn't get any more money because the bank was shut for Hogmanay. As the day's events seemed to have blurred the exact detail, I adopted my best attempt at an appropriate accent and sympathised with yet another atrocity perpetrated by the arrogant interlopers. He narrowed his eyes and squinted me up and down. I knew my efforts had not been sufficient to escape the 'glittering eye' and far from 'skinny hand'. Then inspiration struck. We returned to the bar where a mutual re-canting took place and, taking advantage of a now elaborated version of the story being explained to the barmaid, I took the opportunity to slip away.

The second particular difference I had not anticipated. Nurtured on a view of Scottish New Year by the televised antics of the likes of Jimmy Shand and Kenneth MacKellar, I had booked in at the Castlebay Hotel for New Year's Eve. With the children safely in bed, the adults in the party could enjoy a rare night out, with the appropriate ration of seasonal spirit.

The lounge bar was busy enough, although rather decorous, and I was beginning to think that the public bar, which through the adjoining wall sounded considerably less seemly, would be the better option, when a curious thing happened.

Where there had been noise there was silence, where action, inertia. The locals, one by one, drifted out of the lounge bar, leaving us in the company of a barmaid who, as it turned out, had been instructed to serve the residents, i.e. the two of us, until midnight. Slowly I began to realise the nature of my misjudgement. Unlike the televisual climax of wild-eyed Scotsmen skirling and schreiking as the clock strikes twelve, seeing in the new year in the Western Isles is, at least at its beginnings, a relatively sober affair. The bars in Castlebay close promptly to ensure the Catholic population attends the final church service of the year. Thereafter, any partying that takes place is in the process of first-footing the houses of relations and friends.

So there we stood, eventually joined by the crew of a trawler out of Fleetwood who, as moths, had been attracted to the only remaining light in the building. Even they tired of the lack of action and returned to their boat, where they announced their opinion on matters through disconsolate and increasingly erratic blasts on the foghorn. We were about to go to bed when, in an act of typical generosity, the owner of the hotel invited us to his private family party. In this part of the world, they still regard the passing of the winter solstice not as an excuse for over-indulgence but with a certain amount of relief.

The weather couldn't and didn't last. With the new year came the storms. The picture window in the lounge bar of the hotel was so thickly covered that the outline of Kisimul Castle was scarcely visible. But the spray had not blown off the castle's bay but had been carried by the wind over the island from the west coast. The fact that the source was two miles distant and on the other side of a hill indicated the shape of things to come. There would be no planes landing on Cockle Sands and even the ferry was in doubt. The habit of weighing down the thatched roofs of the black houses with a hair-net of suspended boulders now seemed more practical than quaint.

Several hours late, the ferry steamed into the bay from Lochboisdale. It had now reached mid-point in its circular winter passage around the various outer and inner isles. Passengers from Oban who had been at sea on and off for over ten hours staggered down the gangplank as it struggled to keep contact with the quayside. And they were the lucky ones. The winter timetable meant that those bound for Coll and Tiree (a summer trip of less than three hours) had not only been forced to endure the previous unnecessary leg but had still, at least, another six hours of the Minch before them. I don't know if there is any etymological connection between the terms 'retch' and 'wretched' but there was certainly an actual one on this occasion.

In particular, one elderly couple were on their way to visit their daughter and grandchildren who had moved from the stability of the mainland to the island of Tiree. They had clearly suffered utter misery on the first half of their journey and were steeling themselves for the next leg across one of the roughest stretches of water in the world. As soon as we left the protection of the harbour, the force was upon us. Sitting in the saloon, which apart from the bridge is the highest point of the boat, was an illuminating experience. Such was the roll, that if you looked out of the window your view alternated between a wall of sea and a bank of sky. Such was the pitch, that your stomach violently yo-yoed in contra-motion.

It has always been proposed, no doubt by those who have an advantage in supporting such a proposition, that to each there has been given a special gift. A genetic benison that marks the owner from other men. If this is so, then mine is *bon de mer*. I can be as ill as the next when it comes to digesting a dodgy oyster but I have never been sick at sea. Although I put this down, on the whole, to nature, I feel that nurture has also played its part.

It has always been my habit when the cargo and children are safely stowed to seek the solace of the ship's bar. To comply with the puritanical streak that seems to haunt the Scots at play, this type of establishment is to be found in the least accessible or attractive section of the building or, in the case of a ship, somewhere near the bilges. As any student (either through inclination or circumstance) of the Laws of Physics will tell you, this is the most stable point in an oscillating object and thus gives the drinker a handy advantage over those who, through an aversion to the bouquet of the Traditional Highland Breakfast, are forced to suffer the vicissitudes of life on deck. But there is an added benefit for those who have been genetically modified through regular visits to their local.

Nausea is the signal to the brain that the body is being poisoned and the immediate reaction is an involuntary spasm that rejects the invader. As this, at times, can be less than convenient, the brain can be trained to override the instruction under certain circumstances. One of these is if the toxin in question is alcohol. Provided that you slip in a quick one before the ship makes the open sea, the brain is unable to distinguish between nausea induced by motion or malt whisky. So, to be on the safe side of social acceptability, it, even in the most violent of conditions, does nothing. Ergo, all is plain sailing.

Not so fortunate the particular grandparents visiting Tiree. I don't think I have ever seen anyone look so ill. But, with the worst excesses over and the ferry coming into the shelter of the offshore islands, it appeared that nothing further could go wrong...

(It might be interesting at this point to examine the exact nature of their odyssey. In terms of time relative to distance, the equivalent of their desired journey would be a car ride from London to Oxford. However, let us assume that, because of unprecedented roadworks, they have been diverted up the A1 to Edinburgh, across to Glasgow and down the M6 to Birmingham before reaching the M40 and their destination. In addition, for the vast part of the journey, the motorway resembled an extension of Blackpool's Big Dipper. Such had been the trip from Oban to Tiree.)

After such an epic, surely what remained had to be a bagatelle. But Fate still had one trick to pull out of this particular bag. As the ferry approached Tiree, the Tannoy crackled:

Owing to the prevailing conditions, the captain has decided that it would be unsafe to try to dock at Tiree and we shall proceed directly to Coll. Passengers for Tiree are advised to remain on board and return to Oban. Please retain your tickets and boarding passes. Thank you.

There are times when there is little that can be said and less that can be done.

Nor was this the end of the difficulties and dangers to which the islanders have become habitually accustomed. Although Coll had a relatively sheltered harbour that allowed the vessel to moor, there were further problems when motor vehicles transferred from ship to shore. The exit route was out of the side of the ship via a drawbridge of sufficient width to accommodate a medium-sized lorry and length to extend a few feet onto the quayside. As the swell was still significant, the gangway rose and fell with the movement of the ship so that at one moment it was several feet in the air and at another returning to the concrete with a resounding clang.

Offloading was relatively easy. The driver had to judge the point of fall and use the weight of his vehicle to keep the plank in contact with terra firma for a sufficient length of time to allow the departure. Getting aboard was not so straightforward. A local lorry demonstrated the necessary technique. It positioned itself ten yards or so beyond the point where the gangplank would meet the land. At a prejudged moment, it would, as in a Grand Prix start, accelerate in first gear to arrive at the plank as it made contact with the quayside and, most importantly, with sufficient momentum that the vehicle's weight would be well on board before the swell could relift the plank off the ground. The whole affair had to be carried out at speed – any pussy-footing around would mean the front end could be tipped in the air, with probably considerable damage to vehicle and passengers.

Like most acts of expertise, it looks simple when

done well. The next vehicle was a car and, judging by the vacillation, was not being driven by a local. There were a number of false starts, accompanied by much gesticulation from the ground crew. An audience gathered on the larboard rail, as even the most ill perked up at the thought of a spectacle. The process was simple. The driver waited until the gangplank was lifted three feet into the air, slipped the clutch and accelerated at full throttle towards its guillotine edge, which was then in a precise position to slice the car and its occupants in half. The assumption was that the laws of nature would not choose this moment to rebel and that the plank would fall and be in the appropriate place on his arrival.

But theory and practice are two different animals and, after a couple of half-hearted attempts, the occupants of the car removed themselves and their luggage and took the easier option of the pedestrian route. The car was, I suppose, added to the island's expanding collection. The journey, as far as I can recall, offered nothing further of note and we disembarked at Oban sufficiently late to catch the early train home.

Jura

Jura

For those who are interested in malt whiskies (seven and declining), geese (20,000 barnacle/6000 white-fronted and counting) or even golf, then Islay is the place for them. If your inclination is more to hillwalking, then Yula's isle will hold little of interest but be a stepping stone to the superior Jura. Not that Jura is without its whisky, but the product of the Craighouse Distillery differs considerably from the lighter malts of Bruichladdich or Laphroaig. Its taste and texture aptly reflect the dark and rugged island of its origin, for Jura is surely the wildest and roughest of the Hebridean reefs. I expect the odd goose also strays there, but the lie of the land has tended to keep the mashie and niblick wielders at bay. Even if the wilderness were tamed, with greens shorn and fairways mown, it is probable that the adders, which reputedly outnumber the deer, would be seen as an unacceptable hazard when searching for the sliced ball in the long grass.

And then there are the midges. On an early visit, I

recall drawing the bedroom curtains to check on the weather, as I had hoped for a day on the hill. To my disappointment, the sky was heavily overcast. It was eight in the morning and in the middle of summer but it was as if dawn had yet to break, nor indeed ever would. Then suddenly it cleared or, rather, they did, for the gloom was nothing more than an enormous black cloud of midge that had obstructed the passage of the sun. To the average Englishman, the term 'midge' is synonymous with 'gnat', a matter of little consequence, as in 'strain at a gnat', and so the first encounter with the Scottish vampire tends to be interesting. Fleeing Loch Tulla (*This looks a pretty place to camp.*) with the children still encapsulated in the stricken canvas was my epiphany. Others, no doubt had theirs. Perhaps the sight of four grown men, abandoning their camp at Ardlussa and cramping themselves in a telephone box, was just such an occasion.

Yet, despite the fauna, Jura is a splendid place. If you can overcome the morbid fear that every twisted root of heather is a poisonous reptile and keep moving while you're out – or midge-tight the house when you're in – you should spend a delightful few days.

The major attraction to the tourist are the Paps

of Jura, three conical and distinctive hills that are immediately recognisable from a variety of mainland viewpoints. The major attraction to the hillwalker is the traverse thereof. The best place to start is where the road (there is only one) crosses the Corran River just north of Leargybreck. The river is followed to Loch an t-Siob until the climber can strike up the flank of Beinn Shiantaidh, the first of the Paps. In fine weather, the rest of the route is obvious but not simple. In this case, what goes down must inevitably go up. There is a thousand-foot drop between Shiantaidh and Beinn an Oir and a greater one between the island's summit and Beinn a'Chaolais and the going is not of the easiest, being for the most part pathless and composed of scree. In mist, several false spurs can lead the unwary astray. If this were to happen, it ought to be remembered that Beinn Shiantaidh translates as the Holy Mountain and that your feelings should be best kept to yourself. The easiest way to conclude the eight-hour trip is to descend the third Pap, cross the head of Gleann Astaile and contour under Glas Bheinn to Keils. For the very weary, there is a resting place at Cill Earnadail (an ancient graveyard – open to visitors). For the resolute, the Jura Hotel is less than a mile down the road.

If this challenge does not suffice, then return in May when the Bens of Jura fell race takes place. This starts and finishes at Craighouse and involves the ascent of seven hills including, of course, the famous three. The round has been completed in under three and a half hours. An alternative, for the less energetic, is to walk the only well-defined mountain path on the island. This leaves the road a mile north of the Corran bridge and crosses the island from east to west via Loch na Fudarlaich, before descending to the long deserted hamlet of Glenbatrick. This spot is both desolate and enchanting and hours can be whiled away exploring a coastline that contains lofty caves and perfect raised beaches. At such a moment it is difficult to believe that, with the right connections, you could leave Jura and be in Glasgow is less than hour.

Another unusual feature can be seen from the northern tip of the island. From the vantage point afforded by the cliffs at Port nam Furm, you can look across to the isle of Scarba. The intervening water is the Gulf of Corryvreckan. Water, like snow, can hide a multitude of constructional sins and if some modern-day Moses could momentarily drain the channel, the truth would be revealed. A castellated rock ridge runs from Scarba towards Jura and one of its many pinnacles lies relatively close to the surface. At another point in the chasm is an abyss that plunges three hundred feet below the sea bed. The combination of this rock architecture with westerly winds and a spring tide produces the local phenomenon. The sea begins to boil and a whirlpool is formed that explodes spouts of water into the air. Even at more stable times of the year, the cauldron seems to ferment with menace. It is safe to sail through it at slack water but the timing is crucial, as George Orwell discovered when he nearly lost his life while attempting a circumnavigation of the island.

The author of *1984* had retreated to Jura to finish his last and most renowned novel. At first sight, considering its average rainfall, the Hebrides does not seem a particularly suitable venue for a man suffering from terminal TB. But islands perhaps suit novelists or, at least, those of that ilk who detach themselves from the mainland of conventional wisdom. Islands are also a handy literary device to provide a microcosmic setting for the human condition, in the same way that playwrights from Shakespeare to Pirandello have used the theatrical world as a metaphor for life. Of course, as a structured account of the pros and cons of Jura, I realise that this piece is fast becoming as volatile as the Corryvrecken. So perhaps I should leave such weighty matters of life and death to the members of the golfing fraternity who we left on Islay. After all, it is they who, after the initial drive has petered to a halt, learn to deal with the rough and the smooth, before finally ending up in a hole in the ground.

But if metaphysics is your bent, a much better symbol for Jura, and indeed for so many of these islands still remote from the modern passion for arriving at places before you set off, is its petrol pump. It is not, as elsewhere, adjacent to the road, but perched, instead, on the edge of the quay.

Cliffs of Freedom

The title of this chapter is that of a book by Roscoe Howells. The 'freedom' referred to is, or rather was, the freedom to roam at will around the cliffs and bays of an island. Now that island is owned by the Wildlife Trust of West Wales. Although the Trust does not prevent access, it, in the interests of scientific investigation, restricts the movement of visitors to designated footpaths. The freedom that Howells knew and cherished is no more.

The island is Skomer, situated three-quarters of a mile from the south-west tip of Pembrokeshire. It is a tableland 200 feet high and 750 acres in extent. Its mild climate and plentiful fresh-water supply means that it has been inhabited from prehistoric times and the remains of ancient settlements and field systems are clearly seen. Howells' book tells of this history – the invasion by the Vikings who named the island; how, in the early fourteenth century, it was turned into a rabbit farm to feed the gentry and, finally, the almost mandatory conversion to a sporting estate.

During and immediately after the First World War it was for the most part deserted, except for the occasional foray by locals from the nearby village of Marloes to add rabbit and gulls' eggs to their regular diet.

Such occasions were governed by the weather and sea conditions. Jack Sound, the stretch of water that separates Skomer from Martin's Haven, is a particularly treacherous crossing. A combination of wind and tide can make the journey in a small boat extremely perilous and it was necessary to use boats sufficiently small to be manhandled to a safe beaching. Nor was the danger restricted to craft of this size. In 1938, the steamer Lonsdale, bound for Milford Haven, was running short of coal and the skipper chose to conserve what fuel he had by cutting through Jack Sound rather than go right round Skomer. He collided with some submerged rocks which damaged the steering gear. The tide turned and began to run through the Sound, dragging the Lonsdale with it and, despite all efforts by the skipper and crew, finally wrecked the steamer on the cliffs of Midland.

Even in summer, conditions can change rapidly and any visitor to the island has to be prepared to be marooned for days or even weeks. No doubt this uncertainty added to the allure of the place and to no one more than Reuben Codd. The bulk of Howell's book is a biography of Reuben, the last man to farm on Skomer. As a boy, Reuben would beg time off from his duties on the family farm at East Hook and hang round the fishermen at Martin's Haven, hoping to beg a lift to and from the island. Eventually he knew Skomer's nooks and crannies better than any other visitor, but it was a twist, or rather a series of enlacements, of fate that brought man and island together in a conjunction that became as inevitable and, for them, as calamitous as that of the Titanic and its iceberg.

In 1922 Walter Sturt, a wealthy dentist from Exeter, sold up his extensive practice and bought Skomer island as his retirement home. His wife Violet was of a delicate disposition and it was felt that the mild climate and sea air would be good for her health. Sturt signalled his intentions of long-term occupation by bringing with him a full-sized billiard table and a grand piano.

He was a fine sportsman and as such was welcomed into the Marloes community, or at least its cricket-playing fraternity. His elder brother had

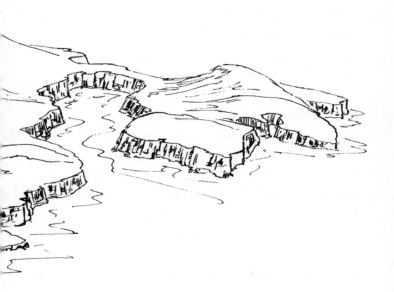

Skomer

played first-class cricket against W G Grace and the requisite genes had not deserted the younger sibling. He was essentially a (very) fast bowler who on one occasion took nine wickets for one run (the last batsman deliberately ran himself out rather than face the whirlwind) and was a sufficiently good bat that the ball had only to touch his pads for the visiting umpire instantly to raise the admonitory finger. But in the end he made a more telling contribution to the local community.

He brought not only his wife but a twelve year-old daughter, Betty. Walter realised that the only way to guarantee fresh milk was to own a cow and Betty was deputed to act as milkmaid. He bought the cow, Snowdrop, from Reuben's father and it made sense that Betty should be sent to the mainland to learn the trade at first hand. It also made sense that Reuben, only three years older, should be her mentor. Eventually the time came for Snowdrop and milkmaid to be shipped, somewhat precariously, to the island in a small open boat. But as the cow was in season, John Codd thought, to ease any future transportation problems, she might as well be put to the bull first.

As months passed, it was clear that the impregnation had been a success, but this posed a further problem. Walter might have been an expert in extracting teeth but calves were another matter. Again Reuben was summoned and once on his beloved island he found every excuse to stay. Children became young adults and the absence of competition led to the inevitable.

Knowing that parental permission was extremely unlikely, they chose to elope. They had no idea how to go about it and one way or another the popular press got hold of the story of a penniless farmhand who had run off with an heiress. They had to go into hiding until a special licence could be obtained but on this occasion fate was on Reuben's side. Bad weather cut off a potentially irate father from any news from the mainland and the first he heard of the marriage was when a journalist asked for his reaction to the union. It was reported that, although shocked and no doubt disappointed at the arrangement, he outwardly accepted his daughter's decision with the same dignified aplomb that he reserved for the more outrageous judgements of the visiting umpire.

As for Reuben, it must have seemed that his boat had come home. Not only had he married into money, but was now in a position to inherit his beloved island. He farmed on the mainland for a while but eventually the siren call of Skomer drove him back. Economically, it was a bad decision, the cost and trouble of transportation far outweighing any advantage, but the island was the island. As Howell opines: *Those who don't understand just don't understand, so it's no use trying to explain to them.*

But then the wheel of fortune started to reverse. World War Two broke out and Betty, for whatever motive, decided to join up and become a civilian MT driver at the aerodrome at nearby Dale. Here she found a social life that she had never previously experienced. No detail is given but this must have been the beginning of the end of the marriage. Also, the war demanded a greater efficiency in the mass production of essential food supplies but the problems of island farming meant that Reuben's attempts to meet these demands caused his costs to rise rather than fall. It wasn't that easy to get a combine harvester onto a little boat.

Once the war was over, Reuben realised that his only hope of economic survival was to develop a particular niche in the market. He tried fattening up turkeys on hard-boiled gulls' eggs, but his eventual solution was to take advantage of Skomer's exceptionally mild climate and put his all into producing early potatoes. His crop would be the first to market and so command a premium price. But, as in the plot of the Hardyesque novel that his story so often reflected, the weather was to have the final say. The winter of 1946/47 proved to be one of the worst on record. I can recall that even in suburbia I opened the door one morning to find the aperture completely blocked by snow. So spring and sowing were substantially delayed.

Nevertheless, Reuben worked around the clock and with his gang of pickers lifted the first crop. However, island farming had its own difficulties. Hundredweight sacks had to be carried from the potato fields to the harbour, loaded onto a small boat and shipped ton by ton to Martin's Haven. Even here, the job was not finished. The sacks had to be lifted out of the boat – much harder work than off the back of a lorry – and manhandled to the top of the cliff, where they were piled up for collection by the potato merchant.

Only after the task had been laboriously completed did the truth, in the form of a telegram, emerge. Because of the late spring, he was no longer ahead of the game. His crop was in direct competition with farms more conveniently situated for moving goods to the centres of population. The market was flooded. There was no call for potatoes from an outpost like Skomer.

Nor was that the end of Reuben's problems. Unlike the mainland farmers who could employ their pickers on a daily basis, Reuben, with the problems of access, had to employ them for the season. If he were to lay them off now, it would be impossible to get them back for the second lifting. If he kept them on, he would be paying men to sunbathe. That was the final straw. He abandoned the project and ploughed the crop back into the earth.

Howells gives no insight into Reuben's reaction to the failure of his marriage and his best laid plans. The plain fact was that he returned to the mainland, never to farm on Skomer again.

My synopsis gives only a broad outline of the problems of island life and *Cliffs of Freedom* should be required reading for anyone tempted to get away from it all. You may not face the problems that Reuben overcame – how to transport a cart-horse across the water, when a moment of panic could result in a hoof disappearing through the bottom of the boat, or reassembling a tractor on the beach of

North Haven in the few hours available before man and machinery were swept out to sea by the incoming tide. But there is no doctor on call, even a visit to the corner shop is a logistical exercise, and you are very much left to your own devices.

Howells recalls picking up visitors who had spent only a few days on the island. Without exception, they would rush to meet the incoming boat full of tales of what they'd seen and done. I understand the feeling. For a week, in pursuit of the more retiring Munros, I spent a period in the wilderness, sleeping rough and surviving on a variety of compositions that bore little resemblance to the picture on the packet. During this time, I saw no one and on the seventh day descended into the valley to meet a friend who was to join me for a quick skirmish above Glen Lyon. We had known each other for many years and our hillwalking norm was single file, some five yards apart and, for the most part, in silence. But on this occasion I couldn't keep quiet and, probably to the annoyance of my companion, continued to chatter all day. Of course, we all live on an island that is bounded by our own existence, but, for the most part, we like it to be furnished with some intellectual and emotional upholstery.

But there is another strand running through the book. In a sense, the author took up the cudgels on behalf of Reuben, who felt that 'his' island had been desecrated by the events that immediately followed the war. Sturt had agreed with the members of the West Wales Field Society that they could use Skomer for research purposes. Reuben watched in horror as hordes of volunteers joined the post-war rush into spectator participation. In this case, it was not watching football or cricket matches but wildlife. Howells' description of events abounds in military metaphor and there is no doubt that he saw the wildlife enthusiasts as an invading army whose intent was to destroy and conquer.

The view the author presents is but one side of the story, but if it is substantially true I can understand his concern. In order for the Society's investigation to have any firm base, there had to be evidence from which opinion could be deduced. The evidence was provided by ringing the birds and clipping the seals. Reuben disapproved of both. To ring birds you have either to catch the adults in nets or the young on the nest before they can fly. The former must be extremely disturbing and the latter counter-productive. As Howells points out, birds build nests to protect their offspring. Either through inaccessibility, narrow ledges, burrows, etc, or through camouflage. If, in the latter case, the nest is the slightest bit disturbed, the changed appearance will be immediately spotted by predators which will investigate with the inevitable result.

In Howell's view, the seals were a more contentious issue. There is no doubt the fishermen of Marloes would have supported wholesale slaughter to retain the level of fish available for netting. In the same way, if for different motives, Reuben tried to cull the black-backed gull which, if allowed to proliferate, could destroy the defenceless flocks of puffins and shearwaters and plunder the nesting places of smaller seabirds for eggs and fledglings. Howells believed that man should take dominion over both the birds and beasts for his own proper purposes (quoting Chapter and Verse to support his argument) but both he and Reuben believed that the same creatures should not be subject to what they saw as idle and misplaced curiosity. They felt, with some reason, that it would be a bitter irony if the only piece of scientific information gleaned from disturbing seals to clip young pups was that, if the mothers are disturbed, they will leave their offspring to die.

What really annoyed the locals was the lack of wildlife knowledge that the professed experts exhibited. At one stage, it was deemed necessary that a new building should be erected to house the Warden and various volunteers. It was proposed that the foundation platform should be made from material already on the island and that the now derelict walls of the old farmhouse should be torn down for that purpose. On the face of it, a sensible way to cut transportation costs. Unfortunately, the walls contained the nests of the rare storm petrel, not to mention hundreds of shearwaters, and the intention was to tear it down during the breeding season.

In fact, it could be argued that the greatest danger to a bird is its self-styled protector. The RSPB has over a million paid-up members and there must be many more who watch birds as a hobby or, at least, take a passing interest in the subject and subscribe to the Society's general aims and objectives. Perhaps in their enthusiasm they can unwittingly cause damage. There was a recent case of an American robin that, through some aberration, found itself in a Grimsby industrial estate rather than its home state of Arkansas. The British Trust for Ornithology spread the news and before long an array of zoom-lenses and binoculars had the exhibit surrounded. A passing sparrowhawk noticed the kerfuffle and took advantage of an early lunch. *It was a terrible moment*, said a member of the Trust, as indeed it may have been. For we will never know whether it was fear or vanity that caused the victim to pose so ostentatiously before the cameras.

I presume the reasons for this enthusiasm are various. It offers a combination of trainspotting, quasi-science and self-congratulation when you announce to your companion: *If you look very carefully at the third bush on the right you will see a Lesser Spotted Wasp Eater* (turdus maximus) *in the act of defecation. Oh dear! You've missed her.* Also, the form and movement of flight please the eye. But, probably, the truth is envy. While we can't run as quickly as the gazelle or swim as gracefully as the dolphin, we are neither the slowest nor clumsiest of creatures at those forms of locomotion. But when it comes to flying, we are entirely dependant on the likes of Icarus Airways.

I once nearly jumped on an eagle. It was hidden under the cornice of a peat-hag, feeding on a dead sheep. I, late for my rendezvous, was running down the hillside, vaulting down the smaller eroded steps. The eagle must have been only aware of me at the last moment because as I took off, so did it. It was one of those slow-motion moments that film makers indulge in. Man in free fall unable to manoeuvre. Very large bird furiously flapping to become airborne. Collision was avoided by a feather's breadth. I watched it fly off and within minutes it had disappeared over the col that was my next objective. As I had to descend and reascend over 500 feet, it took me the best part of an hour to arrive at the same point.

The ornithologist would counter that this is not envy but admiration but, as any tabloid reader is aware, these are two sides of the same coin. Moreover, the admiration can often have an anthropomorphic tendency. The press recently announced the existence of the oldest bird in the world in the terms it had previously used for the oldest woman in existence. She attributed her longevity to a life-long consumption of copious amounts of roast pig fat and vodka (I presume the nineteenth-century equivalent of pork scratchings and bacardi breezers). In the absence of similar avian confirmation, the press paraded as evidence the leg ring fitted in 1957 which, their readers would be amazed to hear, was the year that Harold (birds have never had it so good) Macmillan became Prime Minister. As the bird in question is a Manx shearwater that collects air miles at a rate of 12000 per annum, it would be a bit of a blow to the *Guinness Book of Records* if there were some counter-agency to the RSPB in South America who amused themselves by swapping leg rings around.

Perhaps that's why the shearwaters prefer Skomer: they can count on Jack Sound to keep the enthusiasts at bay for at least six months of the year, which is more than can be said for Grimsby. And there is no doubt it does. I travelled 500 miles in good faith to be greeted by a notice indicating that there was no boat today and the next one was anyone's guess. This was a nuisance but, if you live any distance away, there is no alternative. You can find out when the boat won't be going but there is no guarantee when it will. However, I am in good company. In 1925, the Royal Commission on Ancient Monuments for Wales was unable to include Skomer in its inventory because the inspecting officer was denied access by the weather and, when Walter Sturt bought the island, fog prevented not only access but even a sight of his investment. At least, I was able climb the headland and take the occasional photograph.

Sula Sgeir

Sula

Beyond the barrier reef formed by the Outer Hebrides lies a scattering of small islands that rarely appear on a map of Britain but are, nevertheless, British Isles. Some, like Flannan and Rona, have been inhabited by devout hermits but there are some, without fresh water or soil sufficient to grow the poorest of food, that would have tried the patience of a saint. Such an island is Sula Sgeir, Gannet Rock, little more than half a mile long and at its narrowest point only a few yards wide. In addition, it is surrounded by precipitous rocks and the most dangerous waters in the northern hemisphere. Surely the combined threat of drowning and drought must have deterred even the most hardy. But history says not. In the twelfth century, Bruinhilda, a holy sister of the chapel on nearby St Ronan, must have felt the worldly temptations (e.g. running water) of her mother church to be too great and so repaired to Sula. Here she built Tigh Beannaichte, the blessed house, where she lived and died with only the seabirds as witness.

Nor was she the only visitor to spend time on the rock. From time immemorial, ten men from Ness in the north of Lewis have set sail to the island and once a year ten men still do. It was a great honour to be one of the chosen and the position is handed down from father to son. Until recent times, the forty-mile journey would have been made in an open boat and without a compass. One degree out and the next stop was Greenland. Today, the group hire a trawler to drop them off and, if the weather holds, to pick them up again. But the reason is the same – they are there to harvest the guga, or the young, of the North Atlantic gannet. Even when an act of Parliament protected the bird against human predators, an exception was made for the men of Ness and each year, taking advantage of the best of the bad weather, they leave for Sula to kill and cure their allocation of 2000 young birds.

The trawler anchors in the sheltered creek of Geodha a Phuill Bhain. Here, its tender ferries men and supplies to a rock platform. It is now that the problems begin. Getting the stores, including barrels of fresh water and bags of peat, ashore and dragging them up sixty feet of cliff-face is an achievement in itself, but this is not the moment for self-congratulation. Before nightfall, the beehive-shaped bothies have to be repossessed from the squatting sea-fowl and brought up to spec – that is, waterproofed with tarpaulin and for the most part rendered guano-free. Once that job is done, the various parts of an aerial cable and wooden chute for the easier movement of birds and stores have to be resurrected from their stowage and put together again.

If Health and Safety were to have reservations over the 'machinery', it would be less than happy about the working conditions. The shop-floor is bouldered with perpetually wet and greasy rock, with all the inherent dangers of a consequent broken ankle. The nesting fulmars consistently and automatically vomit over any passer-by. Refreshment, when it arrives, is usually cold and often contaminated by the environment. The method of killing is time-honoured. The group works in teams of three. A, using a spring-jawed pole, catches the bird by the neck and swings it to B, who clubs the head before passing the body to C for decapitation. All this is done with the same rhythmic precision with which their forebears oared the waves or beat the tweed into shape. The tenth man is cook for the day.

This is all fairly straightforward when performed at ground level but eventually the more accessible sites are eliminated and it becomes necessary to slide down the sloping ledges and vertical gullies of the cliffs themselves to reach their target of 200 birds a day. What H & S would make of the workforce dancing from ledge to ledge with the occasional support of a plastic washing line scarcely bears thinking about.

But killing the guga is the easy part. It is after they have been ferried to a more sheltered spot that the serious work starts. They have to be plucked, singed, de-winged and salted before the return journey home. This is a long and complicated process and finishes with the carcasses being built into a broch-shaped mound that guarantees that the preservatives will achieve the maximum effect. Only when all is complete will they allow themselves the indulgence of a guga supper. One bird will feed four men and it has the consistency of steak and the taste of kipper – the ultimate surf 'n' turf. The novice tears at the obvious flesh, while the connoisseur takes the delicacies such as the skin between the claws.

Assuming that a sou'easter is not blowing, the trawler should appear at the appointed hour. As soon as it is seen on the horizon, the exodus begins. First the shelters and then the bird stacks are dismantled and everything is moved to the head of the chute, which slopes down to the landing platform. Bit by bit, barrels, bags, birds and various bundles slide down the chute and are ferried to the mother ship. When everything is safely on board, the chute is taken to pieces and stored for another year.

Once home, the catch is divided. Even the allotment follows its own ritual. The 'beasts' are divided, as nearly as possible, into ten equal piles. To ensure equity, one man looks out to sea whilst another points to a specific pile and asks the 'blind man' for a name. Once each man has his share, the sale begins. Most of the catch has already been spoken for, but there is traditionally a quayside shop for those patient enough to queue. They are sold by the pair and are not cheap but the money the whole affair fetches does little more than cover the cost of the trawler and the necessary provisions and equipment for the expedition. Even though demand far outstrips supply, it seems there are other forces at work than simple economics.

Ridgewandering

It is the habit of the tourist industry to describe Arran as 'Scotland in Miniature'. In the sense that it has mountains, heather-clad glens and offshore islands, this is true. It also, during Glasgow Fairs Week, has a largish spattering of the inhabitants of Scotland's principal if not capital city. But to say that it embraces a synopsis of Scotland's high land is over-ambitious. There is nothing to match the slouch of the Cairngorms, the violent upheavals of Sutherland or the roll of the Borders. Nevertheless, there is sufficient truth in the assertion to recommend the island as an ideal place to discover the difference between the Scottish hills and those in the rest of Britain.

The testing ground for this statement is a traverse of the Arran ridges. They are two horseshoes which are joined by the head at Cir Mhor. The southern surrounds Glen Rosa and stretches from Beinn Nuis to Goatfell. The northern circuit stretches from Cioch na h-Oighe to Suidhe Fhearghas and encloses Glen Sannox. The classic ridge walk avoids Goatfell and is best taken from Beinn Nuis to Suidhe Fhearghas in a south to north direction. If crossed this way, the rock obstacles can be climbed at little more than Moderate standard. However, if the ridge is traversed in the opposite direction, the descent into Ceum na Caillach and ascent of A'Chir can be a couple of grades harder. Both obstacles can be avoided without too much difficulty. Hillwalkers should be aware that under winter conditions the traverse of any of the Arran hills is a very different proposition. The security of rough granite disappears and stretches of Grade III are to be expected.

Assuming that you start from Brodick, a track follows the Glen Rosa Water until a path turns off and ascends alongside the Garbh Allt, which after heavy rainfall lives up to its English translation of Rough Burn. It was in just such conditions in 1901 that a party of climbers set off to examine the great cleft that splits Beinn Nuis. E A Baker and J W Puttrell, with their wives, were visiting the island as a guest of L J Oppenheimer. The three men decided to tackle the cliff head-on, while the ladies under the guidance of Oppenheimer's brother took the path that followed the flank of the hill to its top. An initial inspection suggested that the gully would offer no real difficulty and it was assumed that climbers and walkers would arrive at the summit at about the same time.

The first obstacle was a waterslide of wet and rotten granite. There were no holds and it was only overcome by building a human pyramid, which enabled the top man to scrabble into the gully bed and pull up the other two on the rope. As retreat would have been difficult to accomplish safely, they found themselves in the position of that other local climber, the Thane of Cawdor, for whom 'returning were as tedious as go'er', though in this case the liquid was more hydro- than haemogenic. After an easy stretch, they were again stopped. This time by a steep walled cavern. They deemed this unclimbable after a series of attempts, so tried to bypass the difficulty by escaping onto the face of the cliff itself. Eventually they found a small ledge and that four hours had elapsed.

Meanwhile, the rest of the party had given up its day's walk and was perched on the hillside, anxiously awaiting the outcome. Another three-man pyramid ensued and Baker, the lightest, was propelled onto a shelf which seemed to consist of rotting vegetation held together by bilberries. The rest of the party followed and all gratefully regained the safety of the gully. It seemed that their difficulties were over and for some time they made rapid progress. However, there was a final twist.

They reached a chimney capped by an over-hanging chockstone. All efforts failed and after six hours of being cold, wet and hungry, they called down to their friends to go and get help. They then realised that such assistance would be unlikely to arrive before dawn, so decided on one last effort to branch out onto the holdless granite face. They thought it might just be climbable if it were possible to string together a passage from one bit of vegeta-tion to another. Human pyramids at this point would have been suicidal, so there was a change in tactics. Again Baker, as the lightest, was given the honour. He tied himself to the middle of the eighty-foot rope while Puttrell, tied to one end, climbed as high up the chimney as he could. Oppenheimer, tied to the other, stood at the bottom of the chimney. The plan was that, should Baker fall, Puttrell would jerk him back into the fissure, where Oppenheimer would catch him.

Using every bit of friction that tweed and gran-ite could assemble, Baker inched his way to a point where he could begin to traverse back into the gully above the obstacle. It was here that the slack in the rope ran out. Baker, clinging onto bilberry roots, had no alternative but to untie himself from the middle, haul up one end and tie on again before proceeding. Once in the gully, he could see that there were no further obstacles and as soon as the other two had joined him, they quickly reached the top and set off to forestall the rescue party.

The ascent caused a mixture of admiration at the feat and outrage at the foolhardiness, and such was the reputation of the climb that it was not repeated for fifty years. Even then, it took pitons and étriers to overcome the initial waterslide and it was classified as one of the hardest climbs in the district. Those who are intent on traversing the ridge in a day are probably best advised to ignore this opportunity to gain height and take the path to the summit of Beinn Nuis.

The route from Beinn Nuis (hill of the fawns) to A'Chir (the comb) lies across Beinn Tarsuinn. As its name states, it is a connecting link and offers a mile of easy ground, skirting a number of rock towers. As such, it is a suitable complement for what is to come, as the ideal ridge walk should combine the carefree with the careful. Once the gap of the Bealach an

Fhir-bhogha is passed, matters become more rugged and thought-provoking. The ridge starts to define itself until you are faced with a step over a narrow cleft. This is not particularly difficult and most photographs are posed with the subjects' hands in their pockets.

After you have stepped over this *mauvais pas*, the more serious work begins. The route plunges off the end of the comb and, as with all such matters when viewed from above, looks more difficult than it is. Perhaps this was what was putting off a rather eccentrically dressed bloke who was clearly considering the descent. I say eccentrically because, although it was a warm day, he was wearing breeches and what used to be known as a Norfolk jacket. To complete this ensemble, he was clad in nailed boots.

The latter accoutrement was not in itself all that peculiar. At the time of our meeting, debate still raged in the columns of the climbing press as to the relative advantage of vibram and steel for the all-round mountaineer. Tables were drawn up and points awarded as various circumstances were cited to support one medium over the other, e.g. *Steep Wet Grass: nails 10–rubber 0; Pitch 3, Tricouni Rib: nails 8½–rubber 1.75*. What was peculiar was that the usual proponents of nails were either aged remnants from the Golden Age or, if young, trying to corner the bragging rights, as in 'Had a nice half-hour on The Corner, could well be the first ascent in nails.' My newfound acquaintance, judging by his relatively youthful appearance and reluctance to take the plunge, seemed to fit into neither of these august groups.

We struck up conversation. It appeared that his ambition was to complete the Glen Rosa horseshoe. I intimated that I would probably carry on to Sannox but might spend a bit of time poking around the Rosa Pinnacle on Cir Mhor as I hoped that the half-promised arrival of a friend might offer the opportunity to look at a route or two on that splendid sweep of rock. He seemed surprised at the suggestion: *Cir Mhor? Not much on there worth climbing, is there?* As South Ridge Direct was considered among the best anywhere in the country, I assumed he was joking and with a parting remark, half jocular, half petulant, uttered in a manner that much of the young spend time in perfecting, I descended the twenty feet to a ledge that runs beneath the lip of the rock promontory. This in due course developed into a sort of trench and led to the head of a chimney, which I slithered down to easier ground.

It was when I was at the edge of the chimney that I felt a pang of guilt. If he really was as uncertain as he seemed, perhaps I should wait until he was safely down. So wait I did. No one appeared. I went back along the ledge and still there was no sign. Perhaps he had thought better of it. Still, wiser to check. I reascended the wall and climbed to the highest point on the ridge. Still nothing. He must have got a move on to be out of sight. Probably decided to give it a miss. You can avoid the whole section low down on the west side. Probably see him later.

It was when I was half-way up the slope to Cir Mhor that the weather changed. Short sleeves seemed absurd, 'poking around' the Rosa Pinnacle even more so. Best limit my ambition to an ascent of Goatfell. I reached The Saddle that separates Glen Rosa from Glen Sannox and even that ambition faltered and I dropped below the mist into the valley. It was only then that I began to feel more at ease. He couldn't really have vanished into thin air and if he had slipped, I would have had to have heard something. There are enough apocryphal tales of mysterious happenings on the mountains without my adding to them. Nevertheless, in the Climbers' Bar that evening I couldn't help but keep an eye open, hoping I might catch a reassuring glimpse of an odd cove wearing a tweed suit and hobnailed boots.

For those who cross A' Chir without incident, the way up the south-west ridge of Cir Mhor is straightforward, as is the connecting ridge northwards to Caisteal Abhail. However, it is worth diverting to have a good look at the rock architecture which comfortably holds its own with such celebrities as the summit rocks of the Cobbler or the Cioch of Sron na Ciche. In fact, only some of the hills in the far north west could justly claim to be more imposing.

The ridge from Casteil Abhail is interesting but not difficult until the climber reaches Ceum na Caillich, The Witch's Step. This appears, when viewed from a distance, to be a cleft separating two rock towers in a similar manner to the Thearlaich-Dubh Gap on the Skye Ridge. In fact, it offers nothing like the challenge. The descent into the gap consists mostly of loose gravel and offers little technical difficulty. The ascent of the north side is via a diagonal chimney, followed by an awkward little slab. It is possible to avoid this problem by descending thirty feet down a gully on the west side, where easy ledges allow the ridge to be regained. From here on is a fine piece of hillwalking to the final summit of Suidhe Fheargas, where it is worth pausing to admire the views of the Firth of Clyde. From the summit, descend the northeast ridge until a path is joined that leads down to Glen Sannox.

This makes a long ridge walk and long ridge walks are good. There is a sense of tightrope-walking as the land falls away on both sides and amongst the best there are usually passages that have to be negotiated with Blondinish care. It is generally agreed that the ideal day in the hills should allow you to keep high for a considerable period of time, and thought should be given to finding and exploiting such an opportunity.

I was fortunate in this respect. On my first visit to the Lakes, I was taken up Helvellyn by Striding Edge and I imagined this, my first mountain, to be the highlight of the Lakeland holiday. But the following week, my father announced that, given fine weather, he and I would traverse the High Stile Ridge from Red Pike to Haystacks. Even in those days of plentiful public transport, the logistics were quite complex. We were based at Ullswater, which is fine for Helvellyn but not for Buttermere. The decision was made to take a bus to Keswick, taxi over the Newlands Pass and then bus home from the finishing point at Seatoller. An early breakfast was ordered.

In retrospect, I realise that, although well enough organised, we were not over-equipped. Nowadays any self-respecting National Park Warden would have ordered us off the mountain and onto a clearly signposted lakeside meander. Our map was a fold-out page from Baddeley's *Red Guide to the Lake District* and our compass, a Home Guard War Office Issue which worked quite well if you shook it vigorously enough. I believe I was wearing sandals. As my father was in every other respect a meticulous man, his approach to mountaineering might be best described as cavalier. He and his brother once soloed the Devil's Kitchen, in the rain, by mistake.

On this occasion, the sun shone and all was well-founded. For a small boy it was enchanting. Not one summit but four, views down rocky combes, crags to scramble on, pathways that suddenly narrowed. For some reason, I felt it was much more satisfying than the 'up you go and down again' of Helvellyn, and it was at this point that I transferred the adoration which I had, on a year-by-year basis, reserved for the leading lady of the local pantomime to inanimate lumps of rock and gently-moving scree.

I suppose we all have our favourite ridges and on the odd day when the British weather spoils a day on the hills, naming the Top Ten British Ridges is a pub game we all can play. For what it is worth, these would be mine – in no particular order. Before I begin, I should perhaps explain the self-imposed limitations. First, regretfully, no islands. They seem, no doubt for some perfectly sensible geological reason, to have an inbuilt advantage and the ridges of Skye, Rum, Arran and even Harris would scoop the pool in any merit table and make the game too easy. So British Mainland only. Second, to be of sufficient length that it cannot be easily turned into a circular walk, hence no Snowdon Horseshoes. Third, its elevation must impose itself over the adjoining ground, which rules out Hadrian's Wall. Fourth, it must make a reasonable effort to maintain its height; the traverse of the Paps of Jura is certainly not a ridge walk.

This estimation is clearly extremely rough and ready and leaves the field clear for the definitist. He, or she, could devise a formula where x is the sum of the total descent and ascent, and y is the length of the walk from first to last summit, and for a ridge walk to be a ridge walk it must fall within the parameters

Arran ridges

of an agreed ratio of x to y or, for that matter, y to x. Prof Steinkarten, in his paper on 'The Kurtosisity of the British Uplands: When is a Hill not a Hill?' presented to the Dutch Alpine Society, has done some very useful preliminary work on the subject which the debutant cartographic analyst would ignore at his, or her, peril. I leave the matter to greater minds but diffidently suggest that $\cos \theta$ might come in handy.

But back to my list:

For The Munroist: *The South Kintail Ridge*. Seven Munros in a relatively easy day. Enough said.

For The Arts Lover: *The Malvern Hills*. Easy walking from Raggedstone Hill to the Worcestershire Beacon while you recite chunks of 'Piers Plowman' and hum along with Elgar.

For The Bravish: *The Aonach Eagach*. Though not that much of a walk unless you start at the Devil's Staircase and finish at the Pap of Glencoe.

For The Serious Walker: *The Grey Corries*. All the more so if combined with the Aonachs and Ben Nevis.

For The Antiquarian (and -quated): *High Street*. Not the sharpest of ridges but if it was good enough for the Romans... And from Tirril to Troutbeck has a nice ring.

For The Trusting: *The Farrar Four*. The easiest way to avoid a long return walk down Strathfarrar, and/or being locked in by some petulant gatekeeper, is to give your car keys to someone walking in the opposite direction and hope they can drive.

For The Fed Up with Snowdonia: *The Rhinogs*. And this means the whole ridge, not just the Big and Little Ruffian.

For The Sentimental: *The High Stile Ridge*. For obvious reasons. Readers can, of course, feel free to substitute their own leading lady.

For The Connoisseur: *The Rois Bheinn Ridge of Moidart*. Not a Munro in sight and a railway station at start and finish.

For The Financially Challenged: *On Yr Doorstep Ridge*. Must be within walking distance of home.

In my case, the mighty Kerridge Ridge (K313 as it is known in local mountaineering circles), the Stac Polly of the South. Gawp at the views, including telescopes at Jodrell Bank and the towering towers of Fiddlers Ferry. Marvel at the ancient monuments, etc, etc.

No matter how arduous, all good ridges come to an end and it is usually possible to depart them. This is not necessarily true of islands and it is not only the weather that can cause complications. On the first family visit to Arran it was discovered that booking a return berth for a car was advisable and, in the case of Glasgow Fairs Week, essential. Absence of such meant a further two nights on the island. This did not interfere with any essential engagements, e.g. work/ FA Cup Finals, but still presented a major problem. We were running short of cash and in those pre-plastic days there was little prospect of getting any. We had no recourse but to throw ourselves on the mercy of the erstwhile landlady. As the story was rehearsed and the incipient Orphan Annie coached to burst into heart-rending sobs at the critical moment, further accommodation was acquired on the rather dubious basis of a promissory note drawn on the National Provincial Bank of England.

This solved the major problem but there was still a minor — the purchase of food and drink. The chances of anyone *cashing* a cheque during a Glaswegian holiday weekend was, to say the least, unlikely. A laborious calculation based on free-wheeling downhill left the sum of ten shillings as the critical cut-off point. This, in theory, would provide sufficient petrol to glide to a silent halt in front of the house.

We nearly made it. The M6 was abandoned a junction early to avoid penalty but all spluttered to a stop in the middle of the Cheshire countryside. I followed the telegraph wires until I found a house and explained my predicament and wondered if I could use his phone. He would have none of it. Got out the Roller, drove to the nearest garage and returned me and petrol to mother and child, who were now losing interest in constructing the world's longest daisy chain. I suppose it is superfluous to add that this act of selflessness occurred long before the advent of the grocer's daughter.

The Old Man of Hoy

Hoy

I have to admit that, after the Hebrides, the much anticipated visit to Orkney Mainland was a disappointment. This, of course, is not Orkney's fault. There is no reason why it should live up to my preconceptions of how an island should be. Much of it is quite interesting, but it lacked that other-world sense that you get with the likes of Jura.

My clearest memory of the venture is of a number of particularly large bulls being prodded along the public highway by a variety of rather small children. The whole place had the air of a Warwickshire-on-Sea about it. The relics are interesting – Maes Howe, Skara Brae, that sort of thing – but once you get past the fact that 5000 years ago people were clever enough to devise a sliding bolt to secure their own front door, remnants begin to pall. For the first week, I made do with what I could find and then, in the second, I found Hoy.

The ferry from Stromness to the Bay of Quoys lands you in an ideal spot to explore the north, and better, end of the island. The classic round would include an ascent of Ward Hill, the cliffs of St John's Head, Rackwick Bay (home of the Master of the Queen's Music), then a return to Moaness via the Dwarfie Stane. The latter is a great block of red sandstone which has been hollowed out to form a passage and two chambers. Its origin was probably a burial place, but legend attributes the construction to the local trolls. For my part, I have not dismissed the possibility of an especially large strain of Manx shearwater. To those who study these matters, the pursuit of such speculation can also hold interest.

The highlight of the walk is along the spectacular sea cliffs that stretch from Hellia to Rora, and the highpoint of this is St John's Head, where there is a vertical drop of over 1000 feet from cliff top to sea level. It was first climbed in 1969 by E W Drummond and O Hill. The climbers were forced to abseil to the base, then reclimb the face as best they could. The descent took two days, the ascent five. The Orkneys are notoriously windy and as the abseils are for the most part free, the conditions cause rope-spinning on a grand scale. Now that can be really interesting.

Normally, this turbulent airspace is inhabited only by seabirds and, as I peered over the cliff edge,

I wondered who or what is the traffic controller who determines the flight paths of the various species, as they circle to land or wait for their own take-off slot in their foray for food. If the identity of the director is in doubt, that of the top-gun is not. This is the skua. Rather than fish for itself, it will harry other birds until it forces them to regurgitate their own catch. Size is no object. It will slow down gannets by clinging onto a wing with its beak. If sheep invade its territory, it will drive them off by landing on their head and cuffing them around the ears with its wings. Nor are humans exempt. I had hoped to get near enough for a photograph of a lone bird circling above the cliff edge but was quickly forced into an ignominious retreat. Even that was insufficient. Just when I thought it had lost interest, a swoop of dullish brown would emerge from the cover of the undulating ground and skim an inch or two above my head in a most unnerving fashion. This display of WW2 aerobatics continued for a further two miles. I later heard that a flock had once trapped a man in a cave for several days. Quite Alfred Hitchcock.

The real purpose of the camera was to take some shots of the Old Man of Hoy, another sea-girt pillar, the remnant of a natural arch. Sea stacks, if you wish to visit them, are probably the essence of insularity. You not only have to get on, but also there's no easy way off. What is more, they – or, specifically, the separate stacks of Lee and an Armin in St Kilda – are the ultimate ambition of the avid collector of separate summits in the British Isles. For these stacks are the most elusive of *The Relative Hills of Britain*, aka Marilyns.

To achieve Marilyn status, a summit, regardless of actual height, must have a drop of 150 metres on all sides. That figure has vacillated over the years for a variety of reasons and no doubt will continue to do so. Human erosion and the raising of sea level through global warming are two obvious future culprits, but on-going investigation of the stats will continue to be the main player in any further change. The compiler, in a moment of weakness, included Scafell on the grounds that the drop was 150 metres all round, if you forgot about the rock climbing descent of Broad Stand. There was a suspicion amongst the scrupulous that his decision had been merely aesthetic. Fortunately, intellectual rigour overcame sentimentality and in subsequent editions Scafell has been safely relegated to the class of unmountain. Those who feel unhappy about this should immediately form work parties to excavate a suitable chunk of Mickledore.

Although not even a Marilyn, let alone a mountain, the Old Man was to become the best known piece of rock architecture in Britain. In 1966, the second ascent was performed before the cameras and the Age of Tele-climbing began. Tom Patey, who featured in this and similar extravaganza, holds the whole circus up to inspection in his satirical essay 'The Greatest Show on Earth'. Here he describes the events leading up to a television film of a climb on the sea cliffs of Anglesey. The production was more Cecil B de Mille than *cinema verité*. The set, with its camera scaffolding, riggings of ropes and little men rushing around shouting contradictory instructions, resembled rather more 'a naval dockyard' than Man Unlocking One of Nature's Great Mysteries. What dramatic tension there was lay within the struggle of the climbers to make the route as safe as possible and the pleas of the director to space out the pegs so that he could shoot some *actual* rock climbing. Comic relief was the off-air ad libs that were actually on-air. The curtain fell on a Grand Guignol of mayhem as the climbers divided the spoils of the surplus gear that the BBC had been persuaded to provide.

Somehow, I feel, Tele and The Great Outdoors doesn't quite work. To the uninitiated (proponents would be otherwise engaged in the reality) rock climbing seems to be little more than prolonged moments of inactivity, punctuated with the odd grunt of exertion, and, paradoxically, it doesn't *appear* particularly dangerous. Unlike motor racing, where the likelihood of violent accident is inherent, climbing, when competently performed by experts, offers no such moments of catharsis. In fact, the really exciting shots appeared to be the cameramen swinging around in mid-air or, fearless for their own safety, perched in pursuit of their art on some gull-forsaken ledge. This, of course, appeals to the British audience – the sight of the true amateur, against the odds, outfacing the overpaid and pampered professionals. Eventually the director of Channel X lost interest and the idea faded away. Perhaps it was the absence of suitably arresting titles. Even in an age when the use of 'three alternatives' and 'more unique' is commonplace, there must be a limit to the number of times you can herald a televisual spectacular as *The Last Great Problem.*

Televised hillwalking is even worse. A celebrity (preferably female) is taken in hand by a ghillie/

local landowner/Old Man of the Mountains and shown such parts of the last real wilderness that can be readily reached by landrover tracks. The relevant commentary on the view soon runs out of suitably descriptive adjectives (magnificent/extensive/enchanting) so switches to a slightly breathless conversation on quasi-philosophical matters, punctuated by the overcompensating sound effects of boots scrunching scree or the lonely cry of the solitary curlew. Given the point behind seeking the solitude of the hills, this whole farrago of dollies, spot-lamps and gaffer-tape seems somewhat out of place. Skuas might be a bloody nuisance but at least they stay where they belong.

Macc to Mingulay

Over thirty years ago, a combination of misfortune and over-caution led me to depart the ranks of the car owner. Various encounters with the euphemistically described 'second'hand car and its idiosyncratic habit of breaking down in an evenly interspersed sequence of just affordable chunks of repair, coupled with a general incompetence in matters mechanical, suggested that the only way forward was a seamless transition from one warranty-covered purchase to the next. I was on the first rung of the ladder with a brand new Mini Pickup. Not the most elegant of motors, but, with its canvas hood, quite chic as lorries go. In addition, the Government intended at the next budget to introduce VAT on what had been previously untaxed commercial vehicles. So, for the first and probably only time in motoring history, the immediate secondhand value of a new vehicle actually increased once it left the showroom. With the anticipated profit, I would soon be able to transport my family in a car that had windows, rather than one that resembled a prairie wagon.

So there I was, parked outside the house, waiting to pull away from the kerb, when an inspection of the rear-view mirror showed a transit van some hundred yards behind me. I probably had time to pull out in front of it without too much commotion but, as I was in no hurry, I decided to let it overtake. It didn't. As it was towing a transformer, the combined impetus left a rather mangled Mini that was fit for nothing but scrap. The upshot of this early attempt to dabble in the futures market was that I felt it was both safer and cheaper to employ someone else to do the driving and decided that the existing public transport system was more than sufficient to move the reasonably fit and able from A to B.

Ever one to make a virtue out of a necessity, I paraded this opinion to anybody who cared to listen. It was usually greeted with a certain amount of scepticism: *But how do you get from your front door to the nearest bus stop when carrying the suitcases you need for a week in Lanzarote? It's all very well if you're just going into town for a coffee.* So, in a superior moment (you can turn Lanzarote into a most frightful sneer) I announced that such was my faith in bus, train and boat I intended, *en famille*, to travel the length and possibly breadth of the Outer Hebrides using public transport only.

Having announced the theory, I had then to examine the practice. There are many ways of accomplishing a trip from Macclesfield to Mingulay but I would suggest that the best is to pick up the sleeper at Crewe and disembark at Inverness. The sleeper is the nearest we can realistically get to a 'Beam me up Scotty', and to be woken in your 'refuge' with a quietly served cup of tea is more than a mountaineer can reasonably expect. Inverness is, of course, the wrong side of Britain for an assault on its western promontories, but the country's neck is fortuitously narrow at this point and can be easily wrung by a combination of bus and train to reach Ullapool, the most northern port for the Western Isles.

A more interesting alternative is to walk across this isthmus from Bonar Bridge to Ullapool. It is under fifty miles and can be done either in a determined march or with overnight stops at the various bothies *en route*. Those with a real sense of adventure could disembark the train at Lochluichart and quickstep the miles through the Fannich and Inverlael Forests to the same point. The seriously fit will, I suppose, seize the opportunity to continue their train journey to Achnasheen, then sweep through the Fisherfield Munros and, after a quick brew at Shenavall, traverse An Teallach to Dundonnell whence they could warm down over Beinn nam Ban to catch the Ullapool ferry (if it is running) at Allt na h-Airbhe. However, if the *famille* is *en* the smallish size, it is probably better to rely on the bus. But whatever the journey, you will have to take the ferry to Stornoway. Those who travel carless will have the satisfaction of knowing that they have spent 75% less for this privilege than those bent on exhausting the natural resources of the planet.

The difference between the two halves of the Outer Hebrides is probably more distinct than any other two extremities in Britain, more distinct, say than that between the Geordies and the Cornish and, inevitably, religion lies at the heart of this schism. Whereas the southern isles, which are predominantly Catholic, have an apparently carefree approach to life, the Free Church of Scotland, despite the name, does not encourage such liberalism. The Sabbath is strictly observed. The swings in the public parks used to be chained and padlocked to discourage the young from self-indulgent pleasure and alcohol is still banned in the adult playgrounds. The exception to the latter prohibition is the traveller who requires a drink with his meal. As far as I could gather, if you were prepared to hire a sandwich, the double standard would apply and, judging by the optimistic number of benapkined cutlery strewn across the tables of hotel lounges, this happens with some regularity. Certainly no one asked to examine my ferry ticket.

Despite the efforts of those who opposed, restrictions were lifted and the pressures of commercialism began to tell. But the deeper question as to whether Sabbatarianism is generally a good or bad thing is rarely addressed. A day of rest is essential for those engaged in heavy manual work to allow the weekly wear and tear caused by such activity to heal and recuperate. As many long distance walkers have found out, even though the muscles will recover after a night's sleep, continual walking without rest will cause stress fractures in the bones of the feet which, if ignored, can lead to permanent damage. So, in the days before Trades Union, Sundays were a good thing. The problem was that the Establishment, fearing what work the devil might find, felt a need to organise this freedom and the easiest way was to collect the local congregation together and harangue it from the pulpit as to its past and future behaviour. Today it's called In-Service Training.

The realisation that organised religion was often no more than an unjustified form of control and intrusion into personal freedom meant that it would eventually meet with a wholesale rejection. As with all violent pendulum swings, various parts of the infant disappeared with the ablution. The mind also needs a bit of R & R – perhaps more than is provided by a nightly dose of a good night's sleep. The origins of piety could well lie more in a recognition of this need than in a desire to toady to the All Powerful. The sense of well-being that results from a combination of strenuous exercise and the shedding of stress is known to all hill-goers and they, consequently, try to repeat the process at regular intervals. Bit like Church Going, really.

As Lewis has yet to be concreted over, monuments still abound to remind us of a time when man fully recognised the therapeutic value of ritual. If you stand on the rim of the Outer Hebrides and look west towards the group of islands that form St Kilda, you will probably see nothing but water and sky. But from certain points and at certain times of the year –

that is, at each equinox and solstice – the great rock of Boreray, fifty miles distant, is thrown into relief by the setting sun. All these points along the western coast are marked with a monolith or Calendar Stone that form an interconnected chain of sight-lines, of which Boreray is the outer limit. On the summit of Boreray are the remains of a Druid's house and legend has it that at these four moments in the cycle of life and death the Druid would appear, arms outstretched, like a giant framed by a solar halo, to reassure the islanders that all was behovely and that their obeisance, to whatever mysterious power, had been once more rewarded.

In fact, St Kilda, with its own parliament, language and culture, was the last of the proper British Isles before it, too, was overrun by the European invaders. Once it had been discovered, the very nature of Calvinistic zeal could not allow it to stay in this state of ignorance and slowly but surely converted a happy and successful society into followers of an angst-ridden fundamentalism that is based on the social and emotional needs of a nomadic tribe in the desert. The worst offender was the Rev John Mackay, who insisted that the islanders spent so much time in worship that they had insufficient opportunity to carry out the tasks necessary to feed themselves.

An interesting example of the clash in cultures was the church's curing of the 'eight day sickness'. Generally, the islanders were a healthy lot except for this disease, which killed eight out of ten babies. The infection was caused because the local midwife treated the umbilicus with a mixture of fulmar oil and dung. Once this practice was stopped, the sickness ceased. The islanders attempted to resist this interference with what they regarded as their God's will, but Christian opinion prevailed. I have no doubt that this was regarded as a great success in the suppression of heathen practices but the point of the exercise was probably overlooked. If all the babies had survived, there would have been too many mouths to feed, so some form of cull was essential. Only those strong enough to resist the disease would live and the consequent stock would be strengthened. Whatever the cause, the outcome was that a thriving society withered and by 1930 decided to call it a day.

You leave the desolate northern wedge of Lewis, whose landscape echoes its spiritual underpinning, and as you approach Harris things, at least to the mountaineer, begin to take shape. For the rock climber, there is Sron Ulladale, whose 800-foot crag overhangs the northern extremity of Ullaval, and for the hillwalker, there are the eleven miles of the Clisham horseshoe, which contains the highest point in the Outer Hebrides. For those whose concept of height is relative rather than actual, the southern tip of Lewis offers an abundance. In an area of less than eight miles square lying to the west of Loch Seaforth is a cluster of hills that are sufficiently separate to produce eight Marilyns. Such a bounty must be very tempting to those aspiring to The Marilyn Hall of Fame.

Alan Dawson started the whole thing off. His book *The Relative Hills of Britain* lists all 1542 points separated from any neighbouring height by a drop of at least 500 feet (or, more precisely, the slightly inferior 150 metres) and he invited anyone who had completed the ascent of 600 of such to contact him so that, I suppose, he could make another list. The name of the species and the inflated title of the pantheon seem to suggest that the whole affair borders on the ironic. You could reach the magic number without poking your head over 2000 feet — not exactly mountaineering in the Mallory class. Nevertheless, there are some who are taking it seriously.

Over a hundred have passed the 600 mark since the list was published in 1993 and of those thirty have passed, or are in the process of passing, 1000, and five are within touching distance of completing a full house.

The question is: will the Marilyns become the new Munros? It was regarded at one time that the collection of the latter was a reasonable life-time target for the adventurous hillwalker. The only constraint was to sort out the Cuillin before arthritis set in. A look at a recent list of Completionists seems to indicate that this can be too easily achieved. Both the motor car and a plethora of guidebooks have made the task all the more accessible and you can, without over-inconvenience, polish them off in a decade. The chances are that those who have dunbaggin' will be looking around for a new challenge.

Dawson's list offers just this. There is no need to aim at completion. You can decide on your own subset. An obvious one would be all the Marilyns in Britain over 2500 feet but some would regard this as too Scotland-orientated. Other possibilities are all the Marilyns within a specified area, e.g. Wales or the North of England, or all the offshore peaks that fall within the category. As it is a numbers game, you can invent your own and, for example, strive to sustain a running total of summits which equals your age times ten.

If these possibilities were to catch on, there would be all manner of repercussion. Summit cairns would proliferate, as would guidebooks. Disciples of Wainwright could illustrate and describe the 57 varieties of ascent and descent of Bishop Wilton Wold. Readers could thrill to the travails of conquering mighty Muldoanich (503ft), the Monarch of the Minch. No doubt, there would be some local authorities which would insist on wheelchair access. Anyway, Lewis and Harris have over forty of these protuberances. So, if you're short of something to do on a Sunday...

It was a Saturday when the family expedition left the Bed and Breakfast at Tarbert, the only place where I have had to pay a deposit to borrow a plug for the bath, and set off for a similar establishment at Northton. Here we had planned to spend a couple of days. The bus dropped us at the end of the only road, leaving us to proceed to our destination, Number 7. As we alighted, the rain started to fall. Because I had booked all the accommodation in advance, I had no real idea what to expect. But all had gone well up to now. We arrived at Number 7. It appeared deserted.

I knocked on the door with no response and peered through a cracked window-pane into what seemed impenetrable gloom. Checked the letter of confirmation – Number 7. Rechecked the door. Although slightly askew, the number it displayed was indubitably 7. The rain started to increase in its intensity.

I went round the back and found a lean-to with its door jammed open by a brick. At least it would offer some temporary shelter. A door within seemed to lead into the house proper. Further inspection revealed some indistinct shapes that could have been pieces of furniture and bundles of straw which emitted an odd scuffling noise. Incongruously, the outhouse contained a brand new washing machine and a large chest freezer. The place seemed otherwise uninhabited or, at least, uninhabitable. The rain continued to fall rather more heavily.

Northton boasted no other accommodation and the reason for staying two days was the absence of transport on Sunday. It is at this point in the story that the previously-lectured car owner begins to smile. It would be, of course, a smile that is meant to indicate sympathy but there would be no disguising the flicker of *schadenfreude* that I was up the creek without a Peugeot. Nor was this the end of the problem. My next island hop from Harris to Uist was not by a scheduled ferry but relied on a private arrangement with a Mr MacAskill, who in turn was to arrange a taxi for the ongoing section of travel. The reliance that I had placed on a cheery telephone conversation between Macclesfield and Berneray now seemed a little misplaced, as did the family's faith in the omnipotent tour guide.

It was at this moment that a woman, waving briskly and apologising for her lateness, announced herself as our host. But, instead of turning left towards the remnants of what had been a black house, she turned right and ushered us into a recently built and palatially furnished four-bedroom bungalow. The abode of her forebears had been abandoned and an EU-funded mansionette built next door. For once, the chintz decor and china dolls so favoured by B&B proprietors seemed positively inviting. The rain stopped. The children played on the machair and I was able to purchase a pair of the Harris Wool climbing stockings that our landlady knitted to pass the time while her husband was at sea. Two days later, the last of my doubts were removed when Mr MacAskill turned up in his open boat at Leverburgh and deposited us into a taxi (no doubt owned by another member of the clan) at Newtonferry.

The Uists are in fact three islands, North and South Uist which are separated by Benbecula, but because of their proximity to each other have been joined by causeways into one long strand. In fact, so low-lying is the ground on the east coast that it is perilously close to being an archipelago of several hundred fragments and if current fears on global warming are well founded, it might not be long before this were to happen. Once, while staying at Lochmaddy, I decided to climb the small local hills of North and South Lee. Such is the intrusion of water, it is the only time I have set off for a summit in a diametrically opposite direction to that of the chosen objective.

Our journey through these parts was, for the most part uneventful. The only bit of real excitement was the day and night we spent in a hotel on Benbecula. I was on my way out to join the children who were exploring a nearby beach when I noticed that the lounge bar was, for that time of day, unusually full. Not only that but the occupants clearly weren't locals. There was also a general stir and a suffusion of serious drinking. Curious, I enquired. They were, in fact, tabloid journalists rushed by their editors to cover the story of the moment. Apparently, some circus entertainer with his performing bear Hercules had, for reasons no one seemed to fathom, arrived on the island. Whereupon the bear decided to escape and was reported to be roaming (no doubt slavering at the chops) around the locality. Scenes from *The Winter's Tale* sprang to mind. All, however, was well. Hercules had decided not to scour the locality for edible small children, but to swim out to a nearby islet to avoid this unreasonable invasion of privacy.

The only other matter of moment was when I enquired about the bus to Lochboisdale, the last link in a tenuous chain. The hotel wasn't sure and suggested I contacted the proprietor, which I duly did. It transpired that there was no bus and the fact that a timetable had been published to the contrary was an irrelevance. When I suggested there might be some responsible connection between publication and performance, I was left with the imprecation ringing in my ears, as the phone was unceremoniously and somewhat forcefully replaced on its receiver: *Don't blame me! Blame that bloody woman!* It appeared that the lady in question had recently stated that it was only the failed who travelled by public transport and had, to underline her point, withdrawn the local subsidy. The hotel owner then unobtrusively reappeared, offering the services (at fourfold the price) of one of his kinsmen (who may or may not have been part of the MacAskill fleet of private enterprise).

Once Lochboisdale, the southern port of the Uists, had been reached, I knew that all would be plain sailing. We had learnt from previous experience that the battle with midges and alarm clocks could be avoided by booking sleeping cabins aboard the ferry. As with the train, it meant we could be moved whilst inert. Though, if the weather is good, it is best to be up betimes. There is always a special quality of early morning sunlight moving on the sea. But when it is escorted by porpoises and framed by the backdrop of the Cuillin, it truly provides a transport of delight.

Back once again at Castlebay, with a cottage booked for a week, another holiday begins. Arrangements have been made with the owner of the Castlebay Hotel for the long-anticipated boat trip to Mingulay, the southern terminus of the Maccoutaheb Expedition. The ferry swings into the bay. As always, the land rushes to meet us. The now familiar faces strew the quayside. At last, the sailor home.

Heaval

The Last Upheaval

Watches checked and synchronised. Timing of the essence. To arrive even a second late was to negate the whole exercise. Check batteries. Check spare bulbs. Twenty minutes to departure. Final provisions stored. The explosives and detonating gear checked and rechecked. The arduous journey was behind us, the return not yet contemplated. All was provided for. When you fear to be late, you arrive too early. The moment arrived and we walked out of our temporary abode into the darkness. The rain had stopped. The clouds had started to clear, allowing the stars of the winter sky to break through. After all the doubts, it seemed Fate was on our side.

This scene was not the precursor to a dramatic blowing-up of the headquarters of the enemy's High Command but the result of a family decision to risk the Minch in winter and celebrate the Millennium on the top of the highest hill in Barra. The unnecessary motorised indulgence was driven from North Bay to the previously identified parking place and we easily located the somewhat fragile stile that straddled a vigorous barbed-wire fence. The ascent began. An onlooker would have observed: Young Man in front, Old Man at back, respective wives sandwiched between. Young Man steams uphill like a multi-terrain armoured vehicle. Wives glide in slip-stream. Old Man zigzags laboriously behind. Before long, sandwich goes upsidedown Danish.

A somewhat different picture from twenty-five years previously. Then, as a not so old man, I waved the family goodbye when I set off for the first ascent of the hill that had so attracted my attention as the ferry slid through the cluster of islands guarding the entrance to Castlebay. The offer to join me was politely and not unexpectedly turned down by six year-old daughter but three year-old son, for reasons no longer remembered, left the push-chair in which he had been perambulated to this point in the road and, climbing the then robust stile, started up the hill. I followed. Mother and sister awaited a muddy and disgruntled return at the first stumble. But it was not to be. Of course, walking uphill is in itself of limited interest, yet the enthusiasm continued sufficiently for the spectators to disappear homewards and the climb to be half done.

The second half was more reluctantly accomplished through the strategy of finding craglets to climb and puddles to plodge in. These, together with the tactics of dispensing small peppermint-flavoured sweets (curiously known as TicTacs) on achieving a suggested target, ensured steady upward progress. There was only one moment of crisis, when an attractive but no doubt deadly toadstool was found and about to be consumed. The previous calm tone of paternal encouragement gave way to one of irate panic and, for a moment, tears and a tantrum threatened the whole expedition. Order was restored when the child realised that he could see the house where he was staying – and that he would see it better, and possibly even his mother, from the very top – and, of course, after that it was all downhill so to speak.

Quarter of a century later, it was still uphill for the erstwhile but now fast-fading leader. But kindly stops were taken and the knowledge that the alcoholic TicTac was with the advance party gave the necessary spur. To avoid the crag-strewn prow of the hill, we had moved onto the southern flank and the lights of Castlebay were soon seen at a satisfactory distance below. There, as I had learnt from experience, the bars would have been closed for more than an hour as, unlike the English who for the most part have adopted the festival as an excuse for anti-social behaviour, the islanders return to the privacy of their homes and family to see the year out. I was glad to be part of it. As a half-remembered recognition of the rite that celebrated the start of longer days and stronger shadows, it is, for a few moments, a more solemn time than south of the border, where, if you exclude the baptismal element of Trafalgar Square, there is an absence of any serious ceremony. But it was not long before my private ritual of counting steps in sets of four was broken by a voice announcing that the top was in sight.

Heaval is one of those satisfactory hills that has no false summits and, if approached from the east, has a short but pleasantly airy ridge running along its crest. This quickly leads to the Trig Point and, with what was to be my last significant act of the century, I stepped up onto the summit rocks and gave the OS column the customary pat.

We were in sufficient time to have a small private firework party, finish the substitute TicTac and consume the stowed soup before beginning the countdown. On the stroke of midnight, Heaval Mean Time, mutual well-wishing was offered and accepted among our minor salvo of Champagne and Roman

Candles. At the appropriate fraction of a second later, the sound of a gun was heard, fired in Castlebay as a signal for the bells to ring and the fireworks to begin. It was then we realised that the top of Heaval was an ideal vantage-point. Virtually all the centres of habitation were in view and the displays of Brevig, Earsary, Bruernish, North Bay, Borve, the Isle of Barra Hotel (£75 per ticket), Tangasdale and Castlebay were spread before us, gratis. The night was now so clear that even the pyrotechnics of South Uist and Eriskay were clearly visible.

As the final plumes faded, all that remained was to descend. I let the others go first before, with another pat on the column, I hastened to join them. As we had been the only party on the summit, I had wanted to test the Apostle's version of the ultimate order of things and it was with a sense of private satisfaction that I realised I could now claim that I had been both the last *and* the first, at least as far as this and the previous millennium were concerned. A sense that was quickly brought to earth through an ignominious fall on the inevitable slippery slope. This was getting all far too biblical and the mundane task of looking where I was going rapidly took over from such conceits.

First-footers driving from Castlebay to the east side of the island must have seen our torchlights, as there was a perceptible slowing-down and, in one case, a stopping and reversing as they approached the point where the road reached the mountainside. *(Surely not sheep-stealers? Not at Hogmanay!)* With the fortune that favours the confident, the stile was immediately found and soon we were on our way home, threading the car gingerly through the gathering throngs of men, women and children who strode with purpose to the sound that was the burgeoning ceilidh in the North Bay Village Hall.

Bibliography

Baker, E A: *The British Highlands with Rope and Rucksack* (H F & G Witherby, 1933)

Beatty, J: *Sula, The Seabird-Hunters of Lewis* (Michael Joseph, 1992)

Brown, H M: *Rhum* (Cicerone Press, 1972)

Comunn Eachdraich Bharraidh: *Mingulay, An Island Guide* (Castlebay, 1994)

Cooper, D: *The Road to Mingulay* (Routledge & Kegan Paul, 1985)

Dawson, A: *The Relative Hills of Britain* (Cicerone Press, 1992)

Gaunt, J: *Albion and The Almighty, The Special Relationship* (Caxton Press, 1399)

Griffin, A H: *Still the Real Lakeland* (Robert Hale & Co, 1970)

Haswell-Smith, H: *The Scottish Islands* (Cannongate Books, 1996)

Howells, R: *Cliffs of Freedom* (Gomerian Press, 1961)

Mitchell, W R: *Destination Rum* (Castleberg, 2003)

Murray, W H: *The Islands of Western Scotland* (Eyre Methuen, 1973)

Murray, W H: *Undiscovered Scotland* (J M Dent & Sons, 1951)

Patey, T: *One Man's Mountains* (Victor Gollancz, 1971)

Rixson, D: *The Small Isles, Canna, Rum, Eigg and Muck* (Birlinn, 2001)

Russell, M W: *A Poem of Remote Lives* (Neil Wilson, 1997)

Other books by Graham Wilson

Macc and the Art of Long Distance Walking

Mickey Braddock's Works Do & Other Stories

Shakespeare and the Common Man

Climbing Down

English Rugby: A Game of Two Halves

If you have enjoyed this book and
would like information on any
other Millrace titles,
please get in touch.

Millrace
2a Leafield Road
Disley, Cheshire SK12 2JF

tel: + 44 (0)1663 765080
email: viv@millracebooks.co.uk
www.millracebooks.co.uk

G.R.Dale
May '04